{ Copyright }

{ **Warning** }

Climbing is dangerous
Enthusiasm is no substitute for experience.

This manual is designed to give climbers the skills necessary to stay safe, but rock climbing and mountaineering are inherently dangerous, and so this manual is written for experienced rock climbers and mountaineers only. No one should undertake climbing without the proper training or equipment, and participants must take personal responsibility for learning the appropriate techniques and employing good judgment. I strongly recommend that every climber seek instruction by a qualified professional if they are unsure of any aspect of this manual.

By using the information contained within this manual you acknowledge that the information herein may be out of date or inaccurate, and you agree that the author cannot be held liable for any damage that may be caused following the use of this manual.

{ Contents }

{ Info }

If you have any feedback or questions regarding this book, perhaps where more clarity is needed (such as a diagram), then please contact me at:

andy@psychovertical.com

Also get in touch if you have any new titles you'd like to see, and follow me on Twitter at twitter.com/ psychovertical, where I'll keep you posted about any updates for this or other books.

My website at *www.andy-kirkpatrick.com* also has a ton of articles on technique, skills and assorted climbing obsessiveness!

Unit conversion

The following data should help you convert the units discussed in the text.

1 centimetre = 0.39 inch

1 metre = 1.09 yards

1 kilometre = 0.62 miles

1 kilogram = 2.2 pounds

1 litre = 1.7 pints

{ Thank You! }

This book would not be possible without the help of the following… (in no particular order!)

Dale Bird, Ben Ranson, Matt Grigg, Ali Hodnett, Colin Young, Jennifer Pitcher, Michael Carter, Dave Gill, Edward Shelley, Dave Torr, Matthew Taborda, Tracey Edwards, Bob A. Schelfhout Aubertijn, Charlie Tyson-Taylor, Jasen Jordan, James MacRae, Bernd Limbach, Andy Syme, Mike Potts, Emil Meade, Tim Meek, Daniel Gunn, James Lawson, Keese Lane, Arran Moffat, Tim Bateman, Jonny Robertson, Callum Weeks, Romain Bossut, Stuart Kime, Dominic Makin, Alasdair Lawton, Brendan Gill, Goro Tateno, Hiroyuki Kosaka, Steffen Wiggershaus, Christopher Hudson, Stuart McMurtrie, Ardo Robijn, Russ Hore, Dave Barter, Mari Viitala, Aimee Feenan, Liam Wilton, Jay Leary, Ben Pritchard, David Williams, Marc Kaiser, Roman Bartnik, Guy Buckingham, Aaron Victor, John McNamee, Derek Clemmensen, Stephen Fletcher, James Lucas, Scott Flett, Tony Emsley, Rhys Beddoe, Anthony Darbyshire, Kunal Masania, Kyle Wood, Greg Annandale, Fawksey, Jonathan Iggulden, Robert Bronsdon,

Alistair Benson, Victor Hugo Germano, Sam Sykes, David Lilly, Karlis Bardelis, Paul Reid, Matthew Traver, Tim Jones, Scott Corbett, Olle Hjort, Matthew Munro, Richard Naylar, Andy Lole, Richard B Allen, Stephen Knaggs, Fre, Schalk Steyn, Jake Crumpet McManus, James Snell, Robert Miller, Per Forsberg, Chris Dent, Ben Hunter, Mark Strom, Andrew Cook, Alex Palmer, Martin Langby, Jason Budd, Mark Pilling, Richard Crosby, Nathan Panesar-grix, Jeff Mumaugh, Alexandre Buisse, Stephen Adams, Bjarte Gjerdevik, Mark Roddy, Yann Camus, Andrew Smith, Palásti György, Stig Atle Steffensen, Stuart Duff, Andrew, Kevin Mokracek, James Davidson, Richard Beckett, Simon McCartney, Dave Lambert, Henry Smith, Adrian Villalta-Cerdas, Gabriel Foucault, Michal Büchel, Alwyn Johnson, David Samuel Owens, Steph Meslin-Weber, Jerome Strecker, Mark Collins, Mike McCarthy, Adrian Voss, Cary Bedinghaus, Robert Sharpe, Etienne Lobelson, Maciej Leszczynski, Clive Withers, Andrew McCarter, Steffen Oxenvad, Matthew Kingsley, Steve Wakeford, Chris Bagworth, Roscoe Hart, Alan McIntosh, Adrian Hicks, Stephen Mead, Dave Burn, Jon Lumb, Rhiannon Hollick-Cooper, Nuno Curto, Suzanne F. Stroeer, Simon Mitchell, Geoff Fortescue, Wade Morris, Ian Archer, Steve Mallory, Phil Carrotte, Yann Gautherin, Antony Hill, Menna Pritchard, Ryan Kelley, Sebastian Wilhelm Robert Benque, Tom Mullier, Nicholas Cooper, Alan Lythaby, Oliver Child, Jane Talbot, Chris Tennant, Andy Torbet, Marko Didak, Jeff Roberts, Stephen Nuttall, Tony Wood, Alessandro Reati, Laura Pinyot, Simon Thomas, Erik Sloan, Keiran Appadoo, Steve Murphy, Thomas Penrose, Michael Sanderson, Matthew Bailey, Phil Turner, Ben Phillips, Shahina Patel, Karl Gregory, Steven Greenwell, Matt Hall, Dave Murray, William Roper, Sanne Bosteels, Stephen Hampshire, Zach Wasserman, Tewfik Sadaoui, Michael Ghyoot, Neil Murphy, Patrik Schindler, Philip Olsson, Gernot Goluch, Lynn Marsland, Brian Kimball, Justin Grainger, Andy Dinning, Russell Ouellett, Max Biagosch, Ryan Trefz, Pete Sullivan, Willis Morris, Szu-ting Yi, Paul Lydon, David Stillman, Dennis Berryrieser, Felix Glaser, Ben Lane, John Levesconte, Alex Chenvainu, David Flores, Roy Webb, Matt Lewis, Patrick Subarsky,

Steve Duggan, Nate Redon, Kevin Mai, Sam Harris, Lloydd Williams, Henry Crosby, Lee Horrocks, Kin Hoang, Benjamin Gautron, Jonathan Miller, Calum Harvey, Eddie Brennan, Kitt Hodsden, Susie Stavert, Caroline Phelan, Ryan Santoski, Matthew Lamb, Stephen Komae, Spencer smith, Derek Birch, Francis Hunt, Tom Mallinson, Simon Mcphee, Owen Moore, Sonny Bennett, Iain Parkin, Thomas Baldwin, Caroline Bate, Antony Dowell, Trevor Olive, Paul Diffley, Poul Brix, Stuart Clark, Alastair Humphreys, Kate Tyler, Marshall Ralph, Jack Lawrence, Andrew McIntyre, Lucy Wallace, Andrew Moore, Annebell Huang, Louis-Jack Horton Stephens, Jennifer Cave, Mic Cavazzini, Ted Ekberg, Jonny Hawkins, Massimo Manca, John Smerdon, Christian Rouse, Peter Kirkpatrick.

{ Acknowledgements }

Many of the techniques I write about in this book came from either working it out by myself, or with small clues from books and conversations, while others where learnt from the masters of soloing and big walls, who generously shared their knowledge. These include Pete "Pass the Pitons" Zabrock, Mark Hudon, John Middendorf, Royal Robbins, Erik Sloan. There are also the countless people I talked to along the way, in the Lodge Cafeteria, Camp 4 car park and warm bars in Chamonix, asking for advice, which was always given.

And then there are those who simply inspire in their ability to push the physical and mental limits, including Sílvia Vidal, Steve Schneider, Jim Beyer, Takeyasu Minamiura, Go Abe, Lionel Daudet, Robert Steiner, Mike Libecki, Charlie Porter, Ed Drummond, Steve Bate, Dave Turner, Eric Kohl - and many, many others!

I would also like to give a huge thanks to the amazing Menna Pritchard for making me see this project through, still a big wall virgin, but with the heart and strength of a big wall soloist. Lastly I want to thank all those who have helped me get my words in some kind of order, including Aimée Feenan and Steve Murphy - without you all it would have made even less sense!

To Charlie
1950 - 2014

No, the high wire is not what you think it is.
It is not the realm of lightness, space, and smiles.
It is a job.
Grim, tough, deceptive.

And whoever does not want to struggle
against failure, against danger,
whoever is not prepared to give everything
to feel that he is alive,
does not need to be a high-wire walker.
Nor could he ever become one.

As for this book–
this study of the high wire is not rigorous,
it is useless.

Philippe Petit, On the High Wire
(New York: Random House, 1985)

FORWARD

{ Sílvia Vidal }

Solitude. That great companion that sometimes we look for and sometimes we avoid, depending on the moment and our needs.

Solitude. That great friend and ruthless enemy. She helps you, is with you, involves you. But also, she isolates you, condemns you, excludes you.

There are two types of loneliness, the 'good' one and the 'bad' one. You look for the 'good' one deliberately. The 'bad' one finds you unexpectedly. To be alone or feel alone; that is the question.

To write about solo climbing experiences, to start with, I feel a huge emptiness. Emptiness because of the empty words, the made-up phrases; typical concepts such as solitude, motivation, decision making, confronting doubts, responsibilities, fears – all return …

But straight away, all this emptiness begins to fill up with experiences, emotions, illusions, sensations and anecdotes – which are only that, anecdotes. But they are what allow you to write a story, your story. Personal and non-transferable, like the solo climb, like life itself.

 I would normally write in front of a computer, where the words keep coming to me with more or less guaranteed success. But on this occasion, to write about solo climbing, I have had to use pen and paper. And now, in the early hours of the morning, I realise that I am disturbed by thoughts of the implications of solo climbing.

But now, in between lethargic somnolence and surrounded by silence, I am able to write.

Remembering what silence is; remembering that, without it, I cannot listen. Listen to the river, the glacier, the wind, rocks falling … and feel how the brain travels, transported by that silence, towards remote places full of it.

 After a while, you realise that you do not write but that you are, pen in hand, smiling … and you can feel the cold in those extreme weather conditions and the weight of the haul bag. You remember some of the conversations you had with it: the red one, with horns and a tail. And you remember how it fought with the other one: the white one, with a halo and wings. And as you ask them for silence, to be quiet, with so much noise you could not hear anything, you become aware that you needed to hear in order to understand how much you wanted to be there. Alone

You feel a connection with everything, with the memories, and you come back to the present moment, yet realise you are still connected. And then you realise that the connection was one of the presents that you took with you. And that present is a blessing and a danger at the same time because you know that you will want to play again. A game that is far from innocent but nevertheless, constructive and fulfilling.

That is the solo climb: dream first, act later and keep dreaming; so that afterwards, you can share everything that you have seen and felt, and explain that *silence on the walls tells stories … your story.*

Sílvia Vidal

www.vidalsilvia.com

{ The **Intro** }

"It was a cherished experience. I feel I got the chance to see the inner workings of the grand order of things. In the overall scheme of things, it proves that men can do about anything they want to if they work hard enough at it, and I knew that I could do it . . . and that leads, of course, to a strong suspicion that everybody else can do it if they want to."

- Scott Carpenter, recalling his 1962 Mercury 7

A few years ago a friend of mine called Steve Bate decided to undertake a solo of El Cap. Steve had never climbed a big wall before and had all but given up climbing; the reason being, he'd slowly begun to go blind, having only 10% vision left by the time I met him (he was also a Kiwi and ginger, but you can't do much about that). When he told me what was happening to him, that soon he could be totally blind, I said "wow – you'd better get out to the valley and solo El Cap before that happens" (which was obviously a joke). I didn't see Steve for another six months, but when I next bumped into him and asked what he'd been up to, he said "Oh I've been hauling tyres in a quarry". I thought he'd got himself a job, but it turned out he'd been practising for his El Cap solo. "Who give you that idea?!" I asked (the idea of a blind guy soloing a wall seeming pretty crazy), to which he replied "You did".

Steve soon began asking me questions about the dark art of roped soloing on big walls and, feeling somewhat responsible, I began emailing him answers – well sort of.

I'd learnt to solo big walls the hard way, basically teaching myself by using the limited supply of written resources available. Doug Scott's old book Big Wall Climbing had a little bit of out-of-date information on rope soloing and there were some short chapters in Climbing Big Walls by Mike Strassman and Big Wall Climbing by Middendorf and John Long, but everything was vague, incomplete and sort of required that you already knew how to solo a big wall (I hadn't climbed a big wall with a partner yet, so there was much to learn). Being super keen and motivated, with a real thirst for learning, I started at Millstone Edge, a local quarry, and learnt to aid by myself, which meant learning to solo at the same time. I started by exploring the forces involved and how to move without being too sketchy, using a clove hitch and backup knots. I would get a lift out to the crag on wet-weather days, climb all day (learning so much), and then go home in the dark to ruminate on what worked and what didn't. I made a few mistakes, took a few falls and stripped a rope jumaring on it, but basically built up my walls skills to the point where I could aid up easy routes, slowly but safely.

This time spent training meant that the very first aid route I did was the Shield on El Cap (A2+), a 900 metre wall, where I grappled with what I realise I had yet to learn, but adapted quickly enough in order to succeed. On that trip my partner Paul and I also climbed the Salathe and Pacific Ocean Wall (A4), the result being that I had accrued a solid set of skills for my next visit, when I climbed Iron Hawk (A4) and Lost in America (A4). By this point I had the core skills and could move well on a wall for many days, navigating the thinnest lines, but I wondered how I would cope on my own – the experience being all mine, success or failure unshared?

Being a little too driven and a little too short on time or money to waste a trip to the valley to do an easy route, I chose to make my first foray (also the hardest route I've ever done), a seven day solo of Aurora (A5). When I arrived I bought a Silent Partner (still quite the most exotic piece of climbing kit around), and sat at the bottom of pitch one reading the instructions before setting off. Whilst I sat there, feeding in rope and double checking everything, the legendary Steve Schneider walked past and asked me what I was doing. Steve had climbed many routes on El Cap, but most impressively he had made the first one-day solo of El Cap in 1992, so having him appear seemed like a good omen. "Erm – a Silent Partner" I replied, hiding the instructions behind my back. "Nice" said Steve as he walked on.

On that wall I faced many perils due to my inexperience, getting heat stroke on day one being by far the worst, but I persevered through each set back, moved slowly and kept my mind on the job. When I got to the top I felt that amazing sense of breaking through a barrier within myself, the same feeling I'd had when I climbed the Frendo Spur in winter as my first alpine route, and then again when I soloed the North Face of the Droites. After this climb, this first solo, nothing would be the same (you can only really solo a big wall once, after that you're always kept company with that first experience). Since then I've soloed many walls and attempted many more – warm and cold, over weeks, sometimes days, sometimes in hours – each climb built on the foundation of those early days, alone in that damp quarry.

And so when Steve emailed me I would always give him the briefest of replies, always preferring to point him in some direction where he could learn the answers he sought for himself, just like

I had. I was showing, not telling. I know Steve found this very frustrating, never getting a straight "do this" or "do that", but months later, alone on Zodiac for a week, feeling (and falling) his way up the wall, he finally got it. Soloing is fundamentally about self-reliance, there can be no hand holding, no support or back up, nor pity or sympathy. I would not be there to show Steve the way, he would need to work out all these things from the start – and he did. Almost blind, Steve pulled off his solo.

And so I feel a little uncomfortable writing this book, after all (in many ways), I'm both showing and telling, giving you, the novice soloist, the benefit of all that information so hard won. But then what I have to share is really so little compared to all that there is yet to learn; knowledge that is never complete, but learnt, forgotten, relearnt, adapted, dismissed and learnt again. This book is really only the framework of all that you will need to learn in order to pull off a big wall solo; nothing but a boiler plate onto which you can begin to dream, scheme and plan your greatest adventure.

Andy Kirkpatrick

{ This **Book**}

Someone once told me that when you plan to solo you should just solo, and not hamper that feeling of freedom and unencumbered movement with ropes and gear and gadgets. Soloing should be just that, just your mind and body, a pair of boots and a chalk bag. This free soloing is the truest expression of a climber's freedom, cruising up the rock, but even the best free soloer, pushing their limit, may find a section of the climb where success is uncertain, where a fall would mean certain death. Scale this up to super-long routes and walls, throw in aid sections, or high and low temperatures, routes that may take more than a day, and all of a sudden these things are beyond the free soloist (El Cap has yet to have a free solo ascent, although I guess it's only a matter of time). Here the soloist must begin to employ these tools and gadgets, techniques and tricks, in order to find that solitude, they must invest in the art of rope soloing.

This book is split into three main sections:

Part I: Before the Wall covers all the stuff you need to consider before you go, including gear, training and fitness (more importantly, whether you should be going at all).

Part II: The Wall covers the actual techniques used on a big wall solo: leading, cleaning, hauling and belays.

Part III: Beyond the Wall covers more advanced techniques you may need to learn if you would like to progress onto harder climbs, speed ascents and alpine climbs; basically expanding your skill set to move beyond the big wall solo.

This book is not a general instruction book on big wall climbing and the author expects that anyone reading this book already has an understanding of big wall climbing (aiding,

01

{ Before the Wall }

01 PRE SOLO

There are many things to do before soloing a big wall: planning, strategy, even just getting all your crap there! This section deals with both the big and little things that you need to do before you can get on the rock.

Where to solo?

Before you can solo a wall you need to work out what route to do. I would highly recommend your first solo to be in the Yosemite Valley, as here you have easy access, a mass of beta and solo-bolted belays on many routes; plus, the rock is perfect. By tackling several walls on the Leaning Tower, Washington Column and El Cap you will be able to build up the skills necessary to take your solos to more remote walls. If Yosemite is out of the question, then Norway, the Alps and the Pyrenees or Picos may offer other good routes, but nowhere is as easy as Yosemite (and things will be hard enough anyway).

What kind of route?

The answer to this is simple: STEEP! The steeper the route the easier and safer it will be, as haul bags will be hanging in space and any falls will be clean. Routes with bolted belays are also vital, as this reduces a lot of the weight as you don't need extra protection, and can allow easier fixing and retreat.

For your first wall, routes that are shorter and more technical are ideal with a few ledges preferable, as a ledge allows you to rearrange your gear as well as taking some of the strain out of the unrelenting steepness (they are also simply cool).

Traffic on the route is also a factor, as you don't want to feel rushed, and having teams climbing over each other for days on end can be pain. For this reason I would perhaps leave a wall like the Nose until you have your technique and fitness dialled, and instead look at routes like Zodiac, Tangerine Trip and the Muir or Triple Direct. Routes with some traffic can be nice, as you get visitors now and again, and may be able to beg extra food or water. The famous Chongo Chuck used to 'hitch-hike' up walls by allowing passing teams to fix a rope or two for him and living off their excess food and water. Chongo was also famous for saying that aid climbing was great because you could still be 'bitchin', even while sitting down.

Route planning

When looking at routes, try and build up a picture of the approach, the overall aspect, difficulty and cruxes of the route, as well as the descent. Remember that you will be alone, so it may take two days to get all your kit to the wall and two days to get it back down. Pitchwise, you should try and have some idea of your speed; if you don't, then factor in 1.5 pitches a day, as this will give you a broad margin for error. Get online and look at trip reports (try www.supertopo. com) and google images in order to build up a picture of the route. Get the topo, scan or grab a screenshot and stick it on your phone and computer so you can look at it regularly and build up an idea of the climb.

Plan B

No matter how thorough your planning and strategizing, things don't always turn out quite as you expect them to. Bird bans, rock fall, teams of crazy Koreans encamped on your route, can easily throw a spanner into the works. Have a plan B, even if it's just a topo. For a plan B you may also need a different rack so don't take a specific route rack (say you leave your camalot 5's at home), so take everything you may need.

New kit

If you need to get new kit then buy it and use it beforehand so you're not turning up with brand new gear. However, one item I would always start with as new is a lead rope, and make sure all old kit is up to scratch (cam wires, micro nuts and slings). Being five days in on a wall and having a cam trigger fail or rope sheath come apart is not good for your psyche.

You're not going until you have bought your ticket

So you've done all your planning, bought your kit, told your mates – but you've yet to buy a ticket – well then, you're not going! Buy your ticket as soon as possible so you know you are definitely going; you won't be able to wimp out of it, or find an excuse.

When buying a plane ticket pay close attention to the baggage allowance, as what you save on the flight, you may end up paying for in excess baggage. Another factor is the actual prices for excess. Per kilo prices can be a killer, so price per bag is always better (I was once asked to pay £700 excess when flying back from South Africa with Emirates). Paying upfront online is also worth it and you'd be hard pressed to fly on a plane to solo a wall with less than 50 kg of gear (just a portaledge and fly and rope can put you over your allowance). One option to keep the price down is to take a bike box, snowboard bag or even golf bag and take this on as sports equipment as an extra free item (a portaledge fits in a ski bag well).

Going alone or in a group?
Going on a long trip by yourself can be a great experience, being independent and able to do what you want and when you want is great. Another factor is that going in a group of mates may make it harder to commit to your project, as they may distract you with other plans, or even persuade you to not even try it. If you're already full of doubts, seeing these same doubts in the faces of your mates can break your trip. On the plus side, having your mates there eliminates the loneliness and isolation you can often feel when away from home, which again can be a factor in making you bail. Having people around you to support you and look after you when you get down, to muck in and carry kit to the bottom and from the top, plus keep an eye out for you, cannot be understated. Another positive factor of going in a group is the ability to share the cost of transport, food and accommodation, which can add up when you're alone.

Personally, the majority of my solo trips have been just that, from start to finish. I find that, although it's great to hang out with people I know, it's often hard to break away and get on with the job at hand. People are great but they bring a lot of complexity and personal politics to any situation, and the bigger the group the more of a headache it can be. So the answer to this question will be very personal, but one worth considering.

So you've got your ticket, so now it's time to get there.

02 HOME to BASE

Before you even get to a big wall you will need to transport yourself and all your gear from your home to a base camp. Unless you can drive, you are going to encounter many trials by which impossibility will generally be in reverse proportion to the size of your wallet. Also remember that you are travelling as heavy as anyone can, and this will affect all your timings, so get everywhere early (you can throw money at many things, but not time).

Greyhound Bus

On Foot

A soloist will probably have more than one haul bags' worth of kit to deal with, plus you tend to travel alone, meaning there will be times that you must transport this kit by foot. Travelling with mates will help reduce the stress involved, but there will always be some major lifting and shifting involved. First off, don't think like a cavemen and just try and drag and carry your bags around, as you'll just get injured before you even get there (your bags could weigh 30 kg or more each – 100 kg total baggage is common for a hard wall). What you need is to take advantage of this clever device called 'the wheel'. Using one large haul bag and a super-heavy-duty wheeled holdall that can be pulled works well. You can stick all the heavy kit on the wheels (rack, portaledge, ropes), and all the softer lighter stuff in your haul bag (a ton of light stuff still weighs a ton though). Alternatives include bringing a heavy-duty mini folding trolley (most will not be up to the job), or using a folding kayak trolley (there are many on the market), however, you will need to pack the bag so it's rigid enough to pull along.

If you're using public transport and you can manage it, then try and get a trolley. Most train stations have them, and all airports, but if you're planning on crossing London on the underground, then you're on your own, and are going to undertake an assault course that could bring a hardened SAS veteran to tears (I know – I've done it!).

If you get a trolley, then always put the bags on long ways, not sideways, as this will allow you to navigate lifts, bollards and people much more easily (most of which tend to be a few inches narrower than the bags you have). I also always carry one long kayak roof strap, and use this to lock the bags to the trolley so they don't topple off.

If you have to lift a bag then always try and get some help, and lift from the bottom strap and the top strap.

Trains

As previously mentioned, a trolley makes life much easier when navigating train stations, so make sure you have some change to get one if they are chained together. Haul bags are big items, so aim to avoid rush hour and try placing them in the bike/wheelchair section (but be prepared to move them). If you need to leave them on a platform in order to find a trolley, then make sure you tell someone, as they can look very much like huge fertiliser bombs!

Planes

The days when you could take two huge haul bags on a transatlantic flight are long gone and now most people will get a single bag allowance of around 23 kg, meaning you will need to pay extra for more bags (do this before you fly, as it will be cheaper than just rocking up at the airport and making arrangements). I take this cost now as just part of the price of my flight and invariably end up paying for two extra bags plus overweight charges (most times my bags weigh 30 kg each).

One way to reduce costs is to pay for a ski bag as part of your luggage, or a snowboard bag, and stuff one of these with kit (make sure it has wheels!).

When packing your haul bag secure it as well as you can and consider stowing the shoulder straps as if you were going to haul, but definitely remove the waist belt (these often get pulled off and lost). Avoid using karabiners to secure the bag, as these frequently disappear, but instead secure it in a way that will allow customs to open and check it (at least one of my haul bags always gets checked while going through the baggage system in the US).

Mark your bag with an address, email and telephone number, and try and store all small items, clothes and your rack in smaller bags inside (these can also have your name on), so that if the bag opens, your kit is kept together (you need lots of stuff-sacks anyway).

Automobiles

If you can drive your bags to the wall, or straight to the airport, then this will reduce the hassle greatly. If ordering a taxi, ask for an estate car and tell them that you have some large items, as waiting for a bigger taxi could make you miss your plane or train. If driving a long way, secure your haul bags inside the car (I use a kayak roof strap), as a crash could send a hundred kilos of haul bag into the front seats. It seems crazy to mention it, but also take into account (when really, really overloading your car), that your stopping distance will also be affected.

03 BASE to WALL

Getting all your gear from your camp to the start of the wall can be easy, just load up and ferry your kit in, or it can be the crux of the whole wall. Taking this seriously is vital.

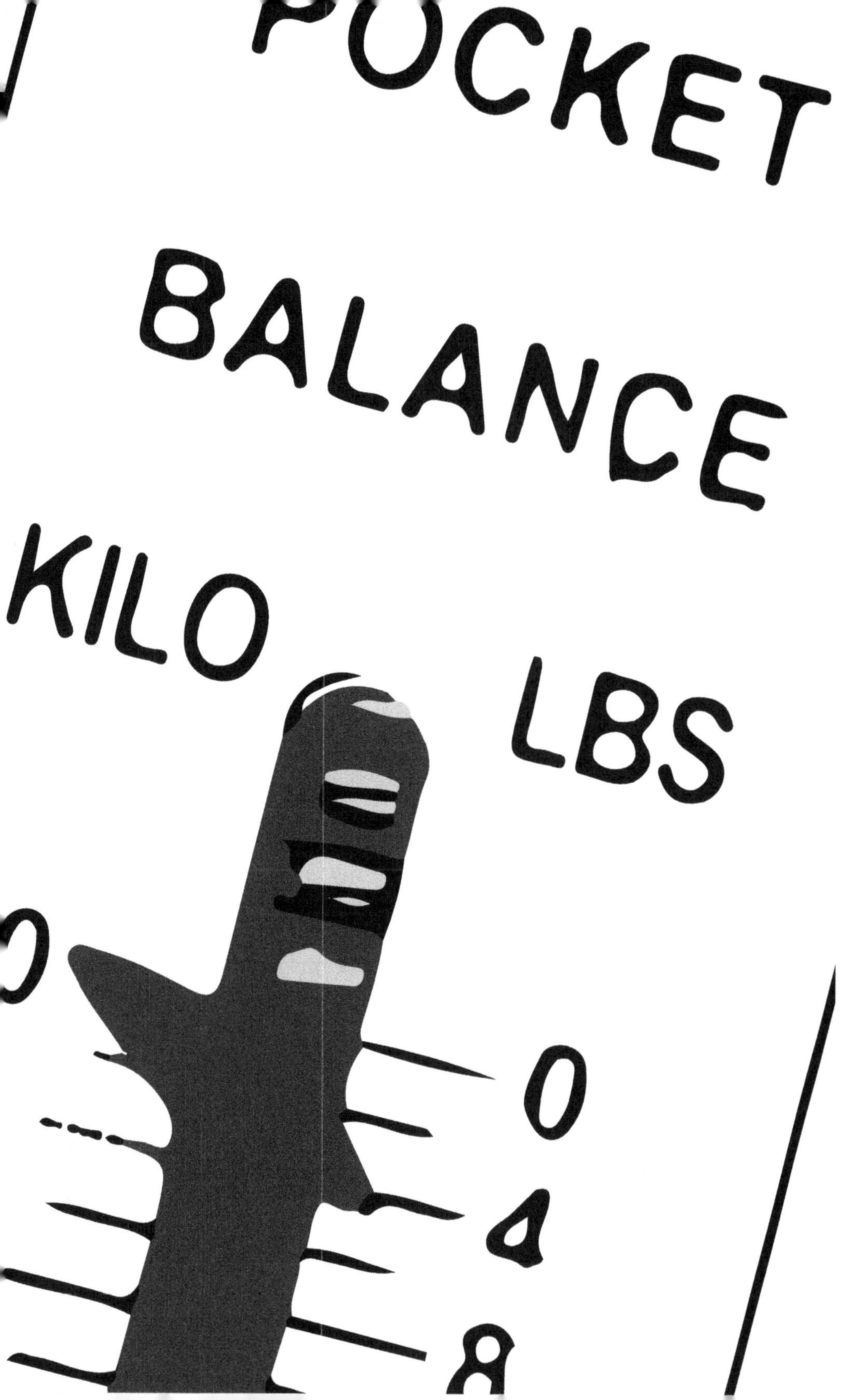
POCKET
BALANCE
KILO
LBS
0
4
8

Man hauling

No matter how good your haul bag is, it will always carry like shit; by far, the best technique used for man hauling, is the ability to absorb pain without complaint. Packing the bag well (heavy items close to the back and hips) will help in some respects, but it will always be a total grind (try and pick walls that are close to the road!).

A better option is to use a super-large pack to haul the kit to the bottom, something in the range of 80–100 litres, as this will be designed for heavy-duty carrying, and although still hard work, should be less painful.

Try and plan load carrying for the coolest times of the day, and for mammoth load carrying, split it up into several carries. Also, don't ignore opportunities to get help from others, even if it's just a couple of litres of water or your ledge. In places like Yosemite you can pay a local sherpa or 'monkey' to carry loads to and from a wall (prices vary, but I've heard $200 is normal). Personally I see this as cheating (although I won't when my knees are shot).

In areas with wildlife like bears, rats, mice or cats, try and avoid leaving your loads on the ground in bags and always make your final carry the one with the food. If you leave a bag sitting below El Cap for example, even if its empty, you'll probably find a bear will rip it open to look inside.

Most walls will be safe from thieves, but not all, and be especially aware of tourists, who will see your gear and assume it's been abandoned. I tend to carry in all the rope and hardware and perhaps the portaledge on day one, and fix one or two pitches, and leave my rack high up at the top of my ropes, then come in on the second day with everything else (or make two carries if I have a lot of water).

One note about your rack: take a moment before embarking on any wall to check each piece of your rack for damage, lubing your cams and paying close attention to your trigger wires (carry spare cord and wire for makeshift repairs). Having a trigger wire fail can create a big problem if you have limited cams.

04 LEARNING

Most climbers don't have big walls on their doorstep to climb and train on, but they still need some way of learning the skills necessary to pull off a big wall solo. This section aims to give you some ideas on how to build up your skills.

Where to start?

First of all it's vital that you have a solid grasp of all general climbing techniques, including knots, devices (GriGri, jumars etc.) and topics such as self-rescue. You will be doing a lot of training by yourself (in fact, all of it will be by yourself), so it's vital that you can operate safely at the crag (set up top ropes, rapping etc.). Next, you should have a thorough understanding of aiding and big wall climbing, ideally having already climbed a few, as trying to learn this while learning to roped solo is asking a lot. I actually learned to do both at the same time – I would go out and practise on bad-weather days, and I knew no one would want to belay me for hours on end whilst I learnt how to do it, but I did make several big mistakes, and came close to killing myself a few times due to a steep learning curve!

I'd also recommend you read up as much as you can from as many sources as possible, from books to the web, as well as emailing or talking to others who may have done it (email is good for getting it from the horses mouth). When I started I didn't know anyone who'd soloed a wall, and could only find two pages in a book that held any information on the subject, so had to make it up as I went along.

The most important thing is your willingness to learn and ambition to climb a wall alone, as well as having patience. You should take each step slowly and learn from everything you do, questioning everything until you understand it (including everything in this book).

You can learn the basics of how to solo at a climbing wall, but you need to get outdoors onto the crag, so that's where we'll start.

Crag training

Almost any crag will do for learning to roped solo, but ideally it should match the kind of rock you plan to solo, so if you want to solo El Cap, then granite or quarried grit is going to work best. Solid cracks are ideal as they will allow you to practise setting up ground anchors, as well as the ability to set up top rope anchors. My practise crag was Millstone Edge in Derbyshire which, although a little loose at the top, provided a lot of great routes to practise on in the rain! Having easy access is also important as you will often be carrying a load of kit to the crag.

When to train

I found that wet-weather days were ideal for training and winter weather adds an extra degree of gnarliness that comes in handy later on during your big wall climbs. Climbing after work in the dark is also good, as the crags are empty and you get a sort of 'other worldly' feel when soloing (just you and your head torch). You can climb on goodweather days, but you often get a lot of stupid questions, people asking you what you're up to.

Looking after the rock

Avoid doing anything that may damage the rock, so no sky hooking or pegging. You can learn these very quickly once you get to the real wall (all simple really, you hammer a peg in until it doesn't come out and hook an edge that holds a hook without popping). You should just use the crag to learn how to move (using aiders and daisy chains) and to work on your solo systems.

Self-lining

If you already know how to aid climb, then I would begin by practising leading but on a top rope – also known as 'self-lining' or 'shunting'.

This is a self-belay top rope, where you fix a stout rope to a solid anchor, then attach yourself to the rope via some kind of ascender, which follows you up the rope. You may already be fully up to speed with self-lining, and if so just jump over this section, otherwise here are some tips on making it work. **Rope:** Use a solid rope, ideally a 10mm static, as this is better able to handle abrasion and heavy wear, as well as not having much 'bounce' when it catches you. Some people would call for the use of a dynamic rope in case the device you're using snags on the rope, creating a loop, thus increasing the chance of a high factor fall (rope catches on device, stops feeding, you climb higher, fall off, you shock-load the device and rope), but I'd argue that if you set it up correctly, and monitor it, then this should never happen. A static rope can take a fall (best not to test this out), but most devices that feature cams can be very aggressive on ropes when shock-loaded.

Anchor: Just treat the anchor like any other, making sure it's 100% secure and that the rope reaches the ground! Some climbers use a double rope system, but I think this is often overkill, plus the extra drag of a second rope can make smooth running difficult.

Belay device: Consult the most current Petzl catalogue for advice on what device to use for self-belaying, however, many climbers use devices such as the Shunt or the Micro Traxion, with the Micro Traxion

being better than the Shunt, as it runs smoothly and cannot be 'grabbed' in a fall (meaning it doesn't lock). The most important factor of which device to use, is how best to attach it to yourself. As with lead solo devices, you need a method that is 100% safe and will not fail due to a twist loading. I would either use a 10 mm maillon or a twist lock oval such as a Petzl OK, wrapping elastic bands on one side to stop the device from going 'off axis'. Once attached, clip this to your belay loop. The Rock Exotica Silent Partner is advertised as being suitable for self-belaying while self-lining, but it's really not very good at all and is best saved for lead soloing (rope feeds very badly).

Backups: When self-lining – as with any roped soloing – you should back yourself up. You can do this in two ways when climbing:
a: Tie overhand knots in the rope as you climb, so that these will block your device if it fails to lock. This is very fast and allows the weight of the rope to help pull it through the device, meaning it is ideal for free

climbing. The downside is that, if the device fails completely and detaches from the rope, the backup will do nothing at all.

b: You tie a figure 8 into the rope and clip this into your harness every few metres. This means that the rope will not feed through the device unaided (you need to pull it through with your hand), but it does mean that if you do have total device failure, you won't fall to the bottom of the crag, just to the backup knot.

Rap device: If you find you need to rap the rope, say you've fallen and are hanging on your self-belay device, then you will need some method of securing yourself to the rope so you can attach a rap device. A jumar and foot loop/lanyard and belay device is the best system, as you can attach the jumar above your soloing device, hang from it, attach rap device, unlatch the belay device and go down (you can also carry two devices, or use one device with your soloing device, and climb up the rope).

End weight: Having a little weight on the end of the rope will help drag it through your self-belay device. A pair of trainers or a pack tend to work fine for this.

When self-lining make sure that the rock above you is 100% solid (especially in quarries), and make sure you wear a helmet and let people know where you're going, just in case you get stuck at the bottom with two broken legs!

Self-lining solo training
With your self-lining system all set up, you should solo a route, ignoring the top rope; everything from building an anchor to leading, placing protection and cleaning. Use the self-lining system both for leading and cleaning, as you can mess up on either when learning (it's easy to end up jumping up on a slack loop of rope held by a single piece of protection, rather than the rope going to the belay).

After a while, you should forget that the top rope is there and you will focus completely on the protection, testing and moving, as well as understanding how the device feeds, when backup knots need tying, and all those little details that can make a big difference once you're doing it for real!

When practising like this I recommend you always take a head torch as time will go by faster than you thought possible, your concentration so focused, it will be dark before you know it!

Leading for real

Once you've got your confidence up with the soloing device, and understand its complexities, you should begin doing some proper ground-up solo ascents. I would recommend doing super-easy free climbs, the type of climbs you'd solo without a rope (the climbing is not the point, the soloing is), further broadening your skills. As you get more confident you can begin to push the grade up, until you should be able to lead routes as hard as you would with a partner.

Multi pitch

Once you feel like you've nailed the single pitch stuff, it's worth scaling it up onto some multi-pitch routes. Again, begin at the lowest grades and expect to take a long time, at least three times longer than normal. Pick easy routes that are less well-travelled, or climb them at unpopular times (for example Tennis Shoe on Idwal Slabs at night). The act of moving on a bigger canvas, dealing with a haul line and lead line, rapping and cleaning, will be invaluable (as well as dealing with rope bags). As before, take it very slowly and avoid any 'oh shit!' moments. You will make mistakes, such as forgetting your jumars, forgetting to clean, crossing over ropes, and maybe even the odd fall, but it should be in an environment that is more forgiving than a big wall. Remember also that most classic routes have very short pitches, often less than 30 metres, so with a long rope you can link two or three together at once.

Training at the wall

If you have a very friendly climbing wall then they might allow you to practise soloing on the wall. To do this you will either need a good ground anchor (check the gyms ground anchors are actually full strength, as some wall's ground anchors are not!) or make one using several weighted bags, or a combination of both. The ideal system would be a three bolt belay ten feet off the ground, so you could hang your haul bag from it and build a proper belay. This would allow you to fully work through leading, rapping, cleaning and hauling. Some walls are open early for maintenance and cleaning and will often let people on 'special missions' come in early, though on a wall you can only really work on systems, rather than the act of self belaying while putting in gear and testing etc.

Hauling training

Practising having bags getting stuck, far-end hauling, and using different hauling systems before you really need them is a great idea. Hanging from a rope close to the top of a wall, trying to remember what I wrote in this book and unstick a bag, is not ideal.

You can practise hauling to some degree at climbing walls, or at crags, but ideally you need a location where you can build a low and high anchor and practise realigning and docking bags, as well as hauling. Hauling a bag full of rocks is great training, but make sure you line your haul bags well with cardboard and a mat, as rocks will wear through the thickest material in seconds if they touch rock.

When practising hauling you should try and focus on:

Releasing the bags: Practise undocking your bags and lowering them out by yourself.

Lowering bags: This sounds easy, but with very heavy bags it can be really tough, so practise lowering your bags down to the lower anchor, or the ground, via a monster munter hitch.

05 THE BODY

They say that in sport, training is 80% physical and 20% mental, while in the actual competition, this is reversed. On a wall, it will feel 100% mental and 100% physical! Soloing a wall will probably feel like the most exhausting thing you've ever done, squeezing every single ounce of energy from your body. By the time you make it down you'll feel like you'll never climb again (it never lasts!).

Training for the wall

Is it necessary to train your body to solo a wall? Well no, and I know many climbers who have soloed walls with no extra training, but often they have climbed many walls before and are already very active climbers. Doing some extra training to deal with the strain of a solo ascent is a good idea, as it will allow you to absorb a bit more punishment, improve stamina and so give your brain a little bit more clarity.

Training/climbing load

If you train at 100% and climb at 50% then you will function well on the wall – a variation on the 'work hard/play hard' idea, being 'train hard/climb easy'. It's virtually impossible to recreate the loading you'll get on a wall, but if you keep up your training day to day, and make it intensive, then you will feel a difference.

The training you could undertake comes in three forms: **STAMINA, STRENGTH** and **SPECIFIC** training.

Stamina

Strength can be a factor on a wall, especially when it comes to hauling, the approach and the descent, but the aspect of fitness that plays the biggest part is stamina.

The grind of leading every single pitch, rapping, cleaning and hauling is tremendous, and the toll on your muscles and joints is heavy. It's therefore well worth trying to build up your overall stamina in the six months leading up to your climb. Doing this helps you recover better after each day, as well as staying on top of things throughout the day.

Here are a few ideas on stamina training:

Running: The most common form of stamina training, running is a good way to build your base, and is free (as long as you've got some trainers). I tend to try and recreate the intensity of the wall by running an hour every day, come what may, allowing my body to adapt to constant training. At the start I can really feel it each time I run, but slowly my body adapts, gets stronger, and although I'm constantly pushing it, it just accepts the aches. This goes against the advice of rest days, but on a wall you don't get rest days, and often your body will be sore from the day before, so getting used to just moving is good.

I'm pretty obsessed with not getting any long-term (or short-term) injuries, so I tend to keep the intensity of runs to a medium level, mixing in hills and flat terrain.

Hill walking: Long days in the hills are ideal for big wall training, as unlike running, they draw on the real source of your stamina, long days grinding you down. I really like setting myself some big objectives, like multiple summits (the Welsh 14 peaks being my favorite), as they require quite a bit of both physical and mental stamina (when you arrive at the last of the hills you'll have to draw on all of your psyche to not give in, just as you will on the big wall). Getting out in the hills at night also helps to increase your ability to keep going (night navigation is great for this), as well as your ability to function under stress.

Weighted hill walks: There is a lot of carrying heavy kit on walls, putting a big strain on your legs and your back. Carrying a weighted pack up hills (do reps on short hills) is a great way to build up stamina and strength in both those areas (your back is asked to take a lot of punishment on a wall). I use large plastic drink bottles (8 litre) that I fill with water and carry up hills, going out for an hour or two (you'll soon get tired). By walking hard you will really feel it in your very core, giving yourself even more of a workout than running. It's vital to save your knees, so I always try and work hard uphill, then empty out the water for the downhill (you can jog down, which looks impressive with an 80 litre pack on your back … who's to know it's just full of empty bottles?!).

Rowing: Although it may seem a little strange sat on a rowing machine (more suited to training for an atlantic crossing), it is one of the best exercises for hard walls and faces. Rowing is low impact yet really builds huge amounts of stamina, both mental and physical. Integrating a 20 minute session on a rowing machine three times a week will result in a huge increase of fitness for a very low outlay of time (but not effort). Your target should be 5 km in under 20 minutes, throwing in the odd 10 km in under 40 minutes every now and then (a real killer!).

Strength

By undertaking several months of intensive stamina training you will naturally getting stronger, but for some people, especially those who don't feel naturally strong, doing some strength work is recommended. Hitting a gym three times a week for just an hour or two will make you stronger, more confident and reduce the chance of injuries.

I would ignore all the fancy machines in the gym, or anything designed to give you a six pack, and instead stick to the simple program.

5x5x5 plus: This regime cuts out all the dead wood and simply means that you carry out five sets of five reps in five core exercises (deadlift, bench press, squat, barbell row, overhead press). The plus part of the name comes from the fact although you are aiming for 5x5 in each session, your actual goal is a little bit more, as often it's giving that extra 10% where you get the physical and mental strength. This means instead of five reps, you squeeze out just one more (five should be a killer anyway), and at the end of your five sets, again you squeeze out one more. Added to this I would throw in an extra exercise for variation in each session to keep it fresh, maybe using kettlebells to hit your heart as well (I personally like T-bar rows, but facing the bar and bringing it all the way up above my head). Going into further details about the exercises I list is beyond the scope of this book, but there is a huge amount of great information on the web (be aware that some information is not so good!).

Doing this routine builds both strength and stamina, without killing you so you can't train a few days later, and only takes an hour or so. A few other points to note:

1. Always warm up by doing the 5x50. 50 star jumps, 50 press ups, 50 sit ups, 50 pull ups and 50 squats (you don't have to do all 50 in one, but make sure you do all 50).
2. Listen to your body and not your mind. If you feel something is not right when carrying out an exercise, back off and use that energy somewhere else. If your mind tells you it's too early, or you're still tired, then ignore it, as once at the wall you'll have no such luxuries.
3. Focus more on doing exercises well than doing them heavy, even if this means the weight starts off a little easier than you like. It's about being in control.
4. Keep notes of weights and exercises in a notebook.
5. Focus on your outcomes and remember what you're training for.
6. Always warm down by running, cycling or easy rowing.

Specific Training

Training specifically for a wall is tough as you can only really do this while on a wall. Nonetheless, climbing is climbing, so the more you do the more this will transfer once you start your solo. One thing that often surprises people when I teach aid climbing is just how physical it is, and so just going through the motions of moving, stretching and lifting will help your body prepare for the wall. Doing sessions at a climbing wall, just going bolt to bolt (as well as hauling), can play a part in developing the strength and stamina you need.

Is any of this necessary?

Big walling takes so much mental strength and toughness that, if you have this already, you can probably overcome a lack of fitness; being fit and prepared can be a game changer when things go wrong and so it's worth the effort, plus feeling fit feeds directly into a positive mental state.

06 THE MIND

Soloing a wall is 80% mental and only 20% physical, which sounds OK doesn't it? Unfortunately I must point out that that 20% physical will be the most physical thing you will ever do, giving some idea of just what 80% mental really means. Needless to say, the mental side of a wall is where most solo ascents are made, or fail, so this section is probably the most important one in this book.

The seed

Before you start, it's worth understanding where the germ on this plan comes from. Why do you want to solo a big wall? Is it based on something you read, or maybe a video you saw on YouTube, a slideshow, maybe even this book? The reason for dreaming is a reason worth understanding, as it may be called on many times – maybe even labelled as misguided or stupid – in the future. This solo seed will probably change as you embark down the path of a solo project, especially your first, as the long road from 'idea' to 'action' will see many waypoints and junctions, taking months, maybe years. In this journey from the source to the sea you may find that, as you learn more about the act of soloing a wall, your motivations might change. Nonetheless, try and remember the seed of this ambition because, when things get hard, it could be the only thing with enough power to keep you going.

What is your motivation?

The ego climber: There are some climbers who simply want to solo a wall for their ego, to be hard core, to live the dream. In my experience, these climbers don't last long, as soloing a wall requires great humility and self-understanding; you need to understand that no one really cares or understands just what it takes to solo a wall, and what kudos you may receive is in no way compensation for what you will give. Within a pitch or two the ego will be pricked and this climber will return to the ground with an excuse.

The quester: The other type of climber is the quester, a person who seeks out personal challenges, who sees and measures themselves as a Spartan, to undertake the hardest trials, be it a triathlon, the Nose in a day, or soloing a wall. This kind of climber is generally very fit, self-contained (they tend to do a lot of self-motivated training alone), and has a good understanding of themselves. If you see yourself as this kind of climber you can flourish on a big wall, but only if you lower your standards a little. The wall is like the sea, it will take all you have to give and swallow you up. Again, humility is important. You may feel indestructible but this will not be a race where you can pull out, there will be no team car to pick you up by the road side. You must temper your strength and stamina and go steadily at 50%, because if you go to hard you may crumble. You can also make the mistake of seeing this as a purely physical game. Yes, you can climb the Nose in a sub-ten-hour time, but alone on a wall, five days in, when a hold breaks and you take a thirty footer onto a copperhead … how psyched will you be?

The wallsmith: This style of climber is one who has spent a great deal of time on the wall, climbing many routes with partners, building up their skills, learning their trade. The wall is respected but also understood, plus they understand their strengths and weakness, and grasp just what an undertaking a solo climb will be. Once this climber understands the specialised techniques required to solo a wall (easy to grasp once you've climbed a few walls), then their climb will unfold without too much trouble.

The overreacher: I've met many such climbers in my time, those who have very little skill at climbing big walls (sometimes none), and no experience at soloing apart from what they have gleaned from books and the web. It could be said that such climbers have developed an obsession with the idea of climbing a wall, be fear they are not good enough to climb one with a partner, and so instead choose to solo one! This style of climber can often be confused with the ego climber, but what they tend to lack – and why they often do well – is any real ego, in fact they often view themselves as crap (which is an advantage on a wall, as they are). These climbers, knowing their severe limitations, will climb slower than most (maybe one pitch a day), and take account of their crapness when working out food and water they'll need to take, meaning they can spend as long as needed on a wall (a self-assured climber may run out of water due to a lack of understanding of themselves).

These climbers will slowly work themselves through the pitches, applying a steady and methodical approach to each little problem and so, in a battle of inches, they tend to do well and often get to the top.

The reason for isolating these 'types' of solo climber is that, in reality, all solo climbers have some element of each type and having a combination of the best attributes will be of great benefit on the wall.

What the ideal solo climber needs

Below is a list of the skills, attributes and experiences that I feel would help a solo climber to pull off their first wall. This list is in no way exhaustive or prescriptive, as many solo climbers who have succeeded have had none of these traits, while others who have failed have had them all!

Humility: You must let go of your ego, and view yourself as nothing; accept that your skills and knowledge are no match for this objective. Begin with the lowest expectations (such as one pitch a day) and build up from that.

Self-awareness: You must grasp what you are to solo a wall, even just a little bit, as you will be alone and exposed to yourself more than any other time in your life. I've met many who are totally nonself-aware, who lie to themselves, remaining closed to themselves and the world. These people do not do well on the wall, or in life. You must understand yourself stripped down to your essence. Once on the wall, the level of self-understanding will increase and your selfexposure can bring great truths about your character as well as darkness (there is nowhere to hide); perhaps this aspect of soloing a wall is what appeals the most and accounts for why people go back. It's also vital that you understand your body and how it reacts to a lack of sleep, reduced diet and the daily grind of being on a wall where everything is down to you. Having undertaken other 'trials' will help in this respect, allowing you to know that when you feel down, or your motivation is waning, it's simply because you need to eat an energy bar ... or have a crap!

Self-motivation: Away from your friends and peers you will need a high degree of self-motivation, as there will be no one there to spur you on, or talk you round. On the flip side, there will be no one to talk you out of it, or de-motivate you (a good and bad thing).

Self-control: Can you wake up at 5am every day and go for a training run? Can you overcome your justifiable fears about dying on the wall, see them as natural, and keep on going? Can you focus on the reason for the fear and press on, without being overcome by it and bailing? A high level of self-control is vital on a wall, both in leading (as with all climbing), but especially when soloing.

Mountain experience: In my experience the climbers who do best on a wall are those who grasp the fact that climbing a big wall is not rock climbing. Alpine or mountain climbing is the same, it has some rock climbing, but is generally much more than that. Instant gratification is not the aim and what you strive for is something more intense and longer lasting. Having some background in climbing in the Alps tends to give climbers that extra grit needed to push on when things stop being 'fun'.

Wall experience: I would advise a would-be soloist to do the basics of an apprenticeship, starting with easy walls, preferably in Yosemite (where you can just 'climb' without all the hassle of mega approaches etc.). Ideally you should develop your skills on such walls to the point where you feel totally comfortable there and know your strengths. On such walls you can ask yourself "could I cope up here alone?" I climbed four walls before my first solo (The Shield, Pacific Ocean Wall, Iron Hawk and Lost in America), but climbing a wall harder than any I had done before probably set the bar too high. It would be better to build up your skills and then choose a wall with a grade lower than what you've already done, such as Zodiac or Lurking Fear.

Self-empathy: In order to survive and thrive on a wall you must develop self-empathy or the ability to love yourself. Now this may sound a little crazy, but the soloist is someone who calls on their body and mind to go beyond what is the norm, placing great strain on every fibre of their being in order to get to the top of a lump of rock. If you view yourself as impenetrable and solid as the rock, you may be able to get so far (viewing yourself like some hero), but slowly cracks will begin to appear and you will crumble. Instead, you allow yourself some measure of self-empathy, not all the time, but maybe each evening, or in how you approach each day.

A good example of this is how, on my first solo wall, Aurora (A4) on El Cap, I wore myself down by trying to climb two pitches every day (leading, rapping, cleaning and hauling), until I was thoroughly wasted. I got so tired trying to stick to this standard I'd set, that I would fall asleep as soon as I lay in my portaledge, or wake up with a half-eaten bagel in my hand.

I was starting in the dark and finishing in the dark. Then one day I dropped my head torch (I found it in a tree when I got down – this was the second time I'd dropped it off El Cap and found it), after which, I was restricted by how long I could climb. All of a sudden I began climbing in the light and had to finish in the light, requiring a much more human approach to myself. I learnt that allowing myself to climb and clean one pitch, but just to lead and fix the next (cleaning it the next day), wasn't so bad. Better still, I suddenly found I was recovering, even enjoying the climb, having time to just chill at the end of the day. The wall became fun, not a race against myself.

I often try and think of myself as someone else I care about (like my mum), and think "what would I do if my mum was soloing this wall?" The bottom line is you need to treat yourself like someone you love.

Selves
The idea of the self is one

I use a lot for soloing. The basic principle is you need to view yourself in the context of past, present and future selves. Each one has an effect on the other and each one owes allegiance to their other selves. In the same way that a climbing team is formed of a number of individuals (and their relationships and support for one another), the same applies to yourselves (or yourselves).

A good example of this comes in the planning of a climb. Ask yourself how well your future self will cope with the objective that your present self is picking? The same applies when picking your food. If you take the time to pick some little treats, caring for a future self rather than just being tough on yourself, then that future self (when the present self), will look back at its past self and be thankful. One useful reason for this approach is that you are often creating things that may not be directly important to you as your present self; you could skip or skimp on things in the present but you are leaving your future self to take up the slack.

Imagine you're leading a thin pitch and you come across a few pieces of protection close together. If you think about your future self you could equalise them all together and form a solid nest of protection so that higher up your future self would feel a little safer… or you could just clip each piece and trust your future self to just keep climbing.

Perhaps the most important use of this concept comes down to being able to press on with the project or the climb. You will feel great doubts about yourself and what you are undertaking, but by looking back at your past self, and trusting that judgement, free of the fear of the present, this may help push you on. There will also be many times, usually early on the climb, when you want to retreat, with the ground still close. On those occasions you must focus on all the hard work and effort of your past self, as well as the disappointment of your future self, that may view retreat in the present as just weakness.

Keeping on going

There will be many crises around a climb, doubts about your plans and dreams, and deep feelings of fear and trepidation; in these moments you need some way of pressing on. One method is to have a mantra that you use in order to ignore the negative, such as "If I keep climbing I will get to the top", or a little story, such as when Royal Robbins made the first solo of El Cap (he almost retreated, but decided to place 'one more piton'), and you recall that that had led to the next one, and the next, until he succeeded and reached the top. My own favourite is perhaps a variation on the 'Invictus' theme of being the captain of my own fate. In it, I visualise an old gnarled hand on the tiller of a small fishing boat tossed around in the ocean. There is every reason why the hand should turn and return to port, but the fisherman is not scared, he understands the sea and stays on course.

Hurdles

There are a number of things that will happen to you on a wall (and on your way to the wall, as well as after the wall), that will stand as hurdles to your ambition. Knowing that others have experienced them before can help, as well as having the self-empathy to accept that they are natural, to be expected. Here is a list of main hurdles you may encounter.

Loss of motivation: There are but a few undertakings that can put so much pressure on a person's motivation than soloing a wall over days or weeks. There will be many ups and many downs, you will feel low at times and want to bail, you will be scared and you will fear you are going to die. All your grand ambitions and dreaming will be nothing in the face of darkness and the storm and there will be times when there really is no valid reason not to retreat. STOP! You must understand that on a solo wall there will be many storms, and clouds as well as sunshine, that will pass across your spirit, but remember that they will pass.

In order to succeed you must never retreat in haste unless it's obvious that you have no choice. Simply stopping and taking stock is always the best option. I think that perhaps the great British obsession with drinking tea lies behind many of its successes, as in tough times people would invariably 'stop for tea'. The process of putting on a 'brew' allows you to take a little breather, to think about things, to allow a little of the pressure to be released. All of a sudden you don't feel that going down easily is the way to go. Remember that you owe it to your past self to not squander the hard work and graft it has put in. Years of planning, a fortune in kit and travel, and days of toil can be undone in just an hour or two if your present self allows itself to crumble and bail. The ability to adopt a high level of self-empathy can reduce this problem greatly.

Keep in mind that 'tomorrow is another day' and what may seem impossible today may seem straight forward tomorrow.

Loneliness: If you're going to solo walls, you're going to have to deal with loneliness. From my experience it seems that people are either born with the ability to operate alone, or they are not. The 'loner' is someone who has always been happy doing their own thing, is selfcontained and self-motivating, something they have done since they were a child. The opposite of this is someone who needs people around them to feel content, needs people to spur them into action, to talk, discuss, laugh and work together for a common goal. A soloist has a common goal, but it is with their past, present and future selves.

I will come to loneliness on the wall, but perhaps the most difficult loneliness comes before the climb, as very often you will be planning, training, traveling and living by yourself. You can be in a hustling place like Yosemite, with hundreds of people around you, laughing and being social, but you are still alone. Often, the more people around you, the more isolated you will feel, and this could seriously jeopardise your chances of achieving your solo climb. I would advise undertaking a solo project within a group of mates, as they will both be company and support (knowing you have mates keeping an eye on you is great, not to mention the fact they can help you lug your kit to the climb).

If you have no support around you then it's vital to get a grip of this loneliness while on the ground. Try and have some escape from your thoughts, like a book or films on your iPad or phone, switching your focus from within to without. Try and stay busy, and be mindful that this isolation is only fleeting.

Fear: Nothing is going to stymie your dreams more than fear, both dreams of soloing a wall and dreams in general. You will not be able to short-circuit your brain to be un-fearful, but through experience and just getting on with it, you will be able to get a handle on it.

First of all you must understand that fear is the like an alarm, set to warn you when there is danger. But who sets the sensitivity of this alarm comes down to you, your experience, and how well you've dealt with fear in the past. By serving an apprenticeship in climbing and walls you are not just building up your skills and strengths, but also slowly turning down the sensitivity of this alarm. The idea of hanging from a sky hook used to terrify me and would keep me awake at night; the first time I actually hung from one (on the Shield), I almost shit myself. But my fear was irrational. I imagined that the metal hook would bend open under my weight, or that the rock would break, but neither happened. Slowly I learnt that hooks were so strong you could take daisy falls onto them (well some styles anyway), and that granite was as hard as steel, and that you could hook edges matchstick thin and they would not crumble. Years later I would lead pitches that comprised of just hooks (such as the crux pitch of The Shortest Straw), and would consider the whole pitch as A1. What I did was retune my mental response to hooks from irrational to rational. By removing the blind fear, I was in fact safer (rushing from a good placement to a bad one due to fear is a prime cause of accidents), and allowed the real alarms to ring when I needed them (for example when a hooking flake was loose).

The simple fact is that in order to climb well on a wall (or on any hard climb), you need to be able to control your fear, otherwise it will just gum up your brain. Try instead to learn how to focus and apply rationality to your fears. Stop and ask yourself "why am I scared?" when you feel the fear rising. A good example is when you rap down your haul line, which is often free hanging. You slide down, your body suspended hundreds of metres up, and you naturally get a frisson of fear. Stop and ask yourself what's the problem? You have a rope that can hold a car, it's attached to solid bolts via sturdy krabs, so what's the problem? In such moments I often try and use the fear as a source of energy, and try and flip it, changing it in my mind from fear to excitement (they are so closely related it's easy to do).

There will be many moments on this journey where you will no doubt encounter fear, from mild fear easily shaken off by an internal 'talking to', to fear so total it will drain the blood from your body.

Identifying and categorising fear

Mild fear: Although the most common emotion for a soloist, this is not fear at all. It usually manifests itself as a background hum of fear – static; people describing themselves as 'worried' or 'scared' about what is to come; the start of the climb; the pitch you must lead 42 tomorrow; committing to a skinny rope running over a sharp edge. The greatest thread from this fear is that it's a Petri dish for negative thoughts and failure. Within this hum of fear you begin to magnify both the danger as well as the task at hand, and the fear just feeds on itself until you either bail before you've begun, or you find the power to overcome it. First off, this is not fear, this is anxiety and it is normal; it is your primitive brain trying to prepare itself for fight, flight or freeze. Like an animal, you are about to enter a situation in which there is a chance you may be killed or injured (after all, you don't feel like this when you walk around Ikea!). It is important to recognise this anxiety and deal with it point by point until you are able to dim it enough to move on. Here are some examples of how this might manifest:

Thought: What if I make a mistake and kill myself?

Answer: I've been training and practising for over year, I've climbed harder single pitches at home, as well as in the rain, storm and darkness.

Thought: I know I've done lots of training, but this would be a real solo on a big wall!

Answer: Think about it rationally, it's just a bunch of single pitch routes one on top of the other. If I can climb one safely, then I can climb them all.

Thought: But what if I get to the crux ten pitches up and I can't do it?

Answer: I believe I can do it and I have all the skills and tools needed to climb that pitch. Maybe it's just one move, who knows, but I know I can do it.

Thought: It's easy to say that now, but what about when I'm up there looking at a huge fall onto a ledge?

Answer: I will place solid gear and test everything. I will equalise runners as I go to make mini running belays. I have offset cams, beaks, stuff they didn't have when these routes where done.

Thought: But what if I can't?

Answer: Then I accept that I may fail and will back off if I think it's not justifiable. Even if I fail, I know it is better to try and fail in the doing of it, not in the thinking of it.

And so this kind of anxiety needs to be dealt with through:

Technical knowledge:
Learning as much as you can about the technical side of this type of climbing;

Technical training: Employing this knowledge in real-world training;

Beta: Knowing your route;

History: Knowing what others have done and the ordeals they overcame helps a lot;

Physical confidence:
Understanding your body and how it will perform;

Faith: Not in God, but in your past ability to deal with problems;

Positivity: Although it's hard, nine times out of ten any situation you worry about will turn out OK, so try and stay positive, even if you only fake it;

Experience: This is the most important one of all. Even if you haven't soloed a wall, I expect you've done a lot of cool stuff in the past that you can draw on. You need a data bank from which you can pull up little 'fear apps' to counter negative thoughts. For example, when you go to lead the crux pitch the next day, think back to how you felt on other climbs and how these climbs turned out.

Perhaps it's only when you experience real heart-pounding fear that you know mild fear for what it truly is ... not fear at all. This kind of fear is unpleasant (it's best not to get into the habit of enjoying it), but is part of the game and needs to be viewed as a sharpener for the senses.

Sharp fear: This is piano-falling-out-of-a-window-and-just-missingyou fear; striking hard and fast, the nature of the close-call determining how long the aftershock lasts. What triggers this response varies depending on experience and what may have you shitting your pants as a beginner (such as a krab shifting as you hang on it), won't even raise an eyebrow a few routes on. The more experienced you become, the faster you tend to deal with a redlining heart and you're able to rationalise what scared you. This is not to say you should totally ignore sharp fear, but in my experience it tends to come after the danger has passed. If it hasn't (a good example being a flake moving when you start climbing on it), then it's paramount that you maintain control in order to escape the situation, be that fight or flight.

Rolling fear: This is the most difficult fear to deal with and is a slowly increasing sense of alarm/danger/deep anxiety that can cling to you for minutes, hours or even days. If you're in this constantly scared state you will not be able to act or think clearly, and worst still, you'll just have a really crap time! The first wall was very much like this for me, as I didn't have the experience to feel comfortable and so blindly pushed on (getting to the belay being my only sanctuary). On a wall, all alone, you could perhaps feel this sense of fear and dread even more, but I think being forced to face these things alone enables you to do a better job of it. The idea of just 'switching off' doesn't work that well, but you can use positive thinking and language to tune out this fear. Instead of viewing the wall as something malign and dangerous – out to kill you – think of it as a crafty opponent, each piece you place (or move you make) a victory in a chess match. Use positive language, such as saying "train stopper" each time you place some good gear. Try and focus on the fun, the adventure, the place – how you're doing something beyond hardcore – that you are thriving and enjoying every minute. Try and have a smile on your face.

Again, think of fear as signals from your primitive and paranoid brain, but don't let them stop you having fun. Out-think the fear.

Failure

You will fail on projects, even some you've spent much mental and physical treasure on. Don't sweat it, it's only natural. When you get to the ground, don't beat yourself up. Getting to the top is awesome, but just getting down safely when you bail is pretty good too – and sometimes getting down is harder Take a moment to feel good about being alive and being capable of getting down alone – a skill that may well allow you to get to the top next time (knowing you can bail is often a vital part in not bailing).

Give yourself a few days to get over retreating and then revisit why you bailed. Was it justified and rational or did you just lose your bottle? Be easy on yourself and remember that what you're attempting to do is very hard indeed. Question your motivation for trying in the first place. Did you grasp how hard it would be? Did you, or the climb, live up to your expectations? Why did you fail and should you try again?

If you come to the conclusion that soloing is, in fact, not for you, then just accept it. Maybe it never will be, maybe it's too soon and you need to do some smaller walls first. Maybe you should just stick to climbing with other people?

07 SOLO TOOLS

The fundamental idea behind all rope soloing technique is that instead of being belayed by a partner, you belay yourself. To stop you in a fall you utilise either a piece of hardware (a device) or a technique (such as a knot). In order to be flexible and adapt to different situations, it's important to understand as many of these methods as possible, as the situation may require you to switch from one to the other. There are several historical systems used on solo ascents that I have chosen to leave out (for example, Charles Cole used a jumar attached to a rope running through his belay device), focusing instead on the core tools, which I have split into knots and mechanical.

KNOTS

If you are new to rope soloing then you should start here, as the use of knots is how climbers soloed routes in the past, and the drawbacks of slowness and inability to pay out remotely mean their use will force you to understand the limits soloing brings. They are also the simplest and safest system for self-belay, and as a foundation skill you may need to call on them at some point in the future when more complex systems fail you.

Clove hitch

By far the best, safest and most foolproof self-belay method for rope soloing on big walls, where the climbing will be predominantly aid. The reason for its effectiveness is that you are always tied into the rope with a knot, and even when loosened, it will still catch you in a fall.

You should already know how to tie a clove hitch, so the next important part is how you connect yourself to the knot. You should connect the knot via krabs to your belay loop, so that the krabs have flexibility and so reduce twisting or cross loading. The knot tends to work best on an asymmetrical-shaped krab, so an oval or HMS would work best. This style of krab, by its nature, is weaker than a D-shaped krab so this must be taken into account. I often use this method on a single HMS when roped soloing during short fixing on speed climbs, but for extended soloing, over days or longer, you need to eliminate the slim chance of breaking your krab in fall (this has happened). To attain greater security you can either double up your connector krabs, say two ovals or two HMS krabs (gates opposed), or employ a steel maillon (a kind of shackle that tends to be more secure than a krab). With either method it's also recommended that you safeguard the locker(s) from spinning around, so as to eliminate cross loading. There are a number of good krabs on the market that feature a system designed to stop cross loading that can work well (such as the Black Diamond GridLock or Rock Exotica Pirate WireEye Auto-Lock); a large krab is also a little easier to handle when using the clove hitch. One krab that may appear to be a winner (but which I find never works well), is the design that features a locking flap (DMM Belay Master), the locker often pops open, or is lost altogether (I would never trust a single HMS using this system alone).

One bonus of using two krabs is that there is a slight decrease in the rope jamming up tight, plus if you do fall, having two krabs allows you to pull the knot apart a little easier.

Once you have tied the clove hitch it can be adjusted with one hand as long as you don't pull it tight accidentally (never place your fingers within the knot when loosening, as they will break, or even be sliced off if you fall while doing so!). The downside of the clove hitch is that on anything but a snails' pace, it's a pain in the arse, so it's worth avoiding micro adjustments and instead paying out a metre or more of slack at a time (or a placements' worth), meaning that after every placement, you pay out enough

slack to make the next.

One variation is to clip a krab into the knot, which will allow you to pull out slack one handed with practise (you pull up a loop,

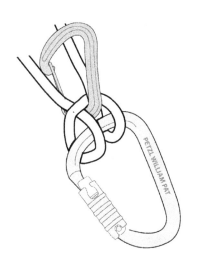

then as you move this loop is sucked back into the knot). The downside is that if this krab was to clip into something in a fall, it could stop the knot from cinching tight (though you will still have your backup knot). The one situation in which this technique works better than the norm is when you're faced with some easy free climbing (you will need one hand free to pay slack), although it's worth practising this beforehand so you understand it's limitations.

The importance of this technique is that, as long as you have a rope, you can use the clove hitch on it. Devices get dropped, or stop working in tough conditions (some don't like ice and snow, which don't affect knots), so having this as a core skills can save your ass.

Figure 8

The figure 8 knot can be used when on easier ground and tends to be tied with plenty of slack, allowing you to make a few moves, then tie another one (you could even pre-tie a number of knots). The downside is that a figure 8 is a tough one to tie one handed and you have to be careful switching between one knot and the other. One way to do this is to use two screwgates back to back, clipping the new knot into one, then the other, then unclipping the old knot in the same style (this means you always have a knot through both krabs). Although used for alpine-style soloing, the figure 8 is of very limited use for rope soloing anything but a few metres (I've used it only once, crossing a rock slab on a solo of the Droites).

MECHANICAL

The modification of existing devices as well as dedicated soloing devices came about due to a need for a self-feeding system, allowing the soloist to both free climb and climb faster. The drawbacks are that these systems are more open to failure, as many are not designed for soloing and expose the user to great risk, they are 'off the grid', plus it's worth noting that they are heavier and more expensive than just tying a knot. Nonetheless, due to need, people have accepted these limitations, feeling these devices still improve the margin of safety. There are several mechanical devices people have adapted for use for soloing, but only three which are actually designed for the job.

'Off grid' devices

By using the devices below, you should fully understand that you are employing a mechanical tool for something way beyond its specifications. It is vital that you understand these limitations and their consequences, as the use of these devices has led to several accidents and many near misses, and perhaps they should be viewed as closer to the solo dictum of "You must not fall" than dedicated, specialised, solo devices (such as the Silent Partner). If using any of these devices it is imperative that you employ a backup knot.

WARNING!
I repeat, none of the following devices are designed for rope soloing or intended to be modified in any way. Any such use or modification is at the owner's risk!

GriGri (unmodified)
Although it's not meant for rope soloing, the Petzl GriGri is by far the most popular rope soloing device on the market (the Mark I is much better than the Mark II, and highly prized), probably due as much to its relatively low price as well as peoples' experience of using it, rather than its safety record as a solo tool (Note Petzl have expressly said DON'T use this device for roped soloing).

The GriGri works the same way as when belaying, locking up when the rope is loaded, only in this situation, the device is attached to the falling leader, not the belayer.

If you use a GriGri all the time then you will fully understand its capabilities, meaning you also know its drawbacks (if you haven't used one, then don't employ it as a soloing device until you've mastered it). On a solo ascent it's relatively easy for the handle to become tangled or snagged and so stop the unit from locking off, meaning you'll fall onto your backup knot. I know of two friends who have had their GriGri fail in this way, one when the rope became wrapped around an arm and so didn't have enough force to lock down the device (resulting in a very deep rope burn), while another had her fifi hooks jam in the device and hold it open. I've used the GriGri a few times and have taken two falls, one that it caught, the other that it didn't (I was saved by an aider clipping into a piece of gear on the way down!). Another problem is that the device can only be attached by one karabiner and unlike a knot, has a good chance of loading the karabiner badly (a British soloist took a monster lob off El Cap a few years ago when the DMM Belay Master attached to his GriGri snapped – being saved by his backup knot). For this reason, when using a GriGri I would use a steel maillon to attach it to my harness and make sure I always have a backup knot, as well as reducing any clutter that could foul the handle (having a chest rig will help keep the amount of gear at harness level to a minimum).

Unlike some of the dedicated devices, it's worth using thinner ropes to allow smooth running and the balance point between your backup knot, device and live rope to be more acute. A GriGri is a highly useful device on a wall, great for hauling and cleaning, so you may have one in addition to a dedicated device, giving you a further option to employ in case you lose your main device.

GriGri (modified)

Some climbers modify their GriGri to allow the rope to feed more smoothly, or attach a loop of cord or wire so they can fix it to a chest harness (the idea is to keep the device orientated in a manner that further improves the rope's ability to feed smoothly). Both involve drilling or filing the device, both of which compound the feeling that you're doing something wrong (again Petzl expressly tell people NOT to do this).

THE MODIFICATIONS

Chest loop: By drilling a small 4 mm hole in the side of the device (and through the plastic base plate), you can thread a loop of cord (3 mm), or wire (it needs to be swaged). This is used to clip your GriGri into a chest harness, sling or bungee, keeping the device orientated in such a way that the rope feeds more easily. The major downside is that, by locking it to your chest, you reduce the likelihood of the device locking in a head first fall (many aid falls are headfirst). By allowing the device to be mobile, you don't restrict its ability to lock.

Rope groove: Where the rope feeds in, there is a flat section of aluminium (the bent over flap of the sliding plate of the device). By filling a more rope-friendly notch (make sure you round off anything you file), you can get the rope to feed more smoothly. The drawback, of course, is that the more easily the rope feeds, the greater load required for the cam to lock (there are no published results for GriGri modifications, so I'm going by my gut feeling). Many of the climbers who have employed this mod are using the device in alpine situations where they have very limited gear, often using ropes far thinner than the spec of the device (8 mm), and are taking the mindset that they are as close to free soloing anyway. Would I make these mods?

I've used modified GriGris as well as unmodified ones and, although sometimes it may

have felt like there was a slight advantage, there's always that niggling doubt that you've messed with something that

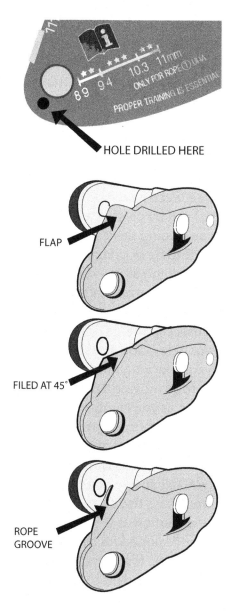

HOLE DRILLED HERE

FLAP

FILED AT 45°

ROPE GROOVE

shouldn't be messed with. I also know many hard soloists who simply use unmodified devices with no problems, so perhaps these mods just come down to tweaking for tweaking's sake, where in fact just getting the know the devices' limitations is just as effective (and a little less risky).

Guide plate
The guide-style auto-locking plate (Petzl Reverso, BD Guide etc.) can be used as a primate rope soloing device, but this tends to be of primary use for those doing alpine soloing with very skinny ropes (again, being close to free solos in mentality). To use, clip the device onto your belay loop as you would in auto-locking mode, with the rope moving through the device as you climb. If you fall feet first, the rope will pull upwards instead of down and the locking krab will catch you; if you fall upside down, it won't. I would use this system with great caution as the device itself is not designed for this type of dynamic force, and really lies in the shady techniques

used by alpine soloists who are aware of just how sketchy this technique is. However, as with all techniques it's worth understanding it, as you never know!

DEDICATED DEVICES
The only company making dedicated devices is Rock Exotica in the US (they traded under the name Wren for a while). They are a highly specialised company making all sorts of strangeness, but the quality of what they make is unquestionable, and I've taken lobs (some very long) onto every one they make.

Rock Exotica Soloaid
The Soloaid is best described as a mechanical clove hitch, allowing a climber to grab slack more easily as they climb. It's also small, compact and relatively cheap, and provides a great degree of security. I used one of these when trying to solo a new winter route on the Troll Wall and, although it was great for aid, when it came to free climbing (I switched to the

Rimmon route), it was a non-starter. A plus point is that the device works if you fall head first, but perhaps it's best to just stick with a clove hitch.

Rock Exotica Soloist
The Soloist probably has the best pedigree of any soloing device and has been used on many of the big solo climbs of the past two decades, including all Catherine Destivelle solos (Eiger, Dru and Matterhorn), Jeff Lowe on Metanoia on the north face of the Eiger, and many other big walls around the world. This device, unlike the Soloaid, allows free movement with no self-feeding required, a boon for those who need to climb free. Unusually, the device is tied to your harness through the leg and waist loop (I use a double loop of 7 mm rope), meaning that you eliminate a weakness by removing the karabiner from the system. A rope (10 mm works best) is placed inside the device, which is basically a block of milled alloy with a slot milled out of

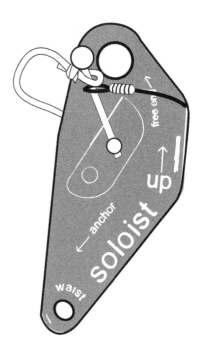

it, and locked in place by the cam, which is held in place by a thick pin. This pin is then locked in place by the karabiner used to hold the device to a chest harness, creating a system that is very secure. The rope feeds through the device very smoothly and if you develop a good understanding of your backup knot loop/live rope ratio, then you can climb close to your limit. In a fall the cam works like a GriGri (it is not sprung though), locking down on the rope, but unlike a GriGri (due to the enclosed nature of the cam), it's virtually impossible for the cam to be fouled, snagged or tangled. The big problem with the unit, as with the GriGri, is that it won't work in an upside down fall, which is a pretty big problem, as it's very easy to take upside down falls when aid climbing. The chest harness is designed to reduce this problem, but this drawback will always be in the back of one's mind when using it. It's worth noting that, although the GriGri has many drawbacks, it should lock in a head-first fall if unattached to a chest

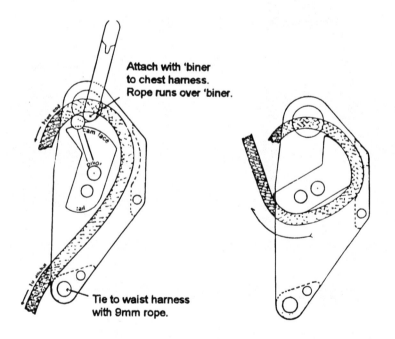

Attach with 'biner to chest harness. Rope runs over 'biner.

Tie to waist harness with 9mm rope.

harness. Luckily the Soloist has been superseded by the Silent Partner and really only has a place (along with the GriGri) for winter soloing, where it has the advantage of having less moving parts and is therefore less prone to freezing up.

The Silent Partner

The pinnacle of mechanical soloing devices, perfect for aid or free, safe in any kind of fall, and used on solos such as Hans Florine's ascent of the Nose and Half dome in a day!

The Silent Partner is best described as being like the locking mechanism in a seat belt; it will run smoothly until you pull too fast, at which point it locks. This mechanism is inside a polished steel barrel, around which a clove hitch is tied. The barrel rotates, allowing the knot to run, then locks down as soon as you pull too fast. The strength of the unit, both in the way it's designed to be used (attached by two krabs) and its simplicity (nothing to snag and foul it), makes it the best soloing device by miles.

History: The Silent Partner was designed by Mark Blanchard, a Yosemite climber and soloist who found the usual clove hitch method too slow for harder free climbing. He played around with the idea of having a clove hitch tied around an inertia wheel, producing a prototype in the 1980s and used by Steve Schneider during his first one-day solo of El Cap's Nose. Mark soon realised that selling such an advanced product exposed him to being liable for its misuse and so sold the design to Rock Exotica (who already had the solo belay device sewn up with their Soloist and Soloaid). Unfortunately for big wall soloists, Rock Exotica was then bought by Petzl, and so the design disappeared for many years, only appearing again when Rock Thompson (the owner of Rock Exotica), set up Wren to market the device (since then, Thompson has split Rock Exotica from Petzl and now sells the Silent Partner again).

How it works: The concept is based on the humble seat belt, which is designed to allow the webbing to be pulled out at a slow speed, but lock when shock-loaded (however, in this case the webbing is replaced by a rope). This inertia wheel is set within a thick steel drum, which is set within an alloy frame that can be twisted open for access. To use, you first tie a clove hitch in your rope and slip this over the drum, which due to its rotation (it rotates both ways), stops the knot from locking. This means the rope feeds smoothly, allowing free climbing and aid to take place with very little maintenance of the device. The device is attached to your harness via the belay loop using two locking krabs set back to back. In a fall the drum is rotated quickly causing it to lock, which in turn locks the clove hitch and voila ... your ass is saved!

The beauty of the Silent Partner is:

• It has no cam aggressively biting down on the rope, but instead is locked by a knot;
• The device works in any direction (up, down, sideways), meaning it will lock in a head-first fall (a Soloist or GriGri may not);
• As long as you tie a clove hitch, the device is almost foolproof,

and will lock even if the rope is secured incorrectly (it will lock if pulled tight in either direction). The downsides with the Silent Partner are:
• It's quite bulky;
• It's probably not a good choice for sub-zero conditions (as the inertia wheel may freeze).
Overall, there is nothing on the market that comes close to functioning so well.

Thoughts on attachment of the Silent Partner: The device is secured using two locking krabs in order to provide redundancy and security. Some have questioned the need for two krabs, but having just one would be highly dangerous, as in a fall it would be easy for the device to load a single krab dangerously (even though most modern krabs are designed to take it). Others feel it wastes time to do up two krabs, but again, it only takes a few seconds (if you want to really save time then use a locker and a plain gate). In the past I've wondered about using two maillon links instead of krabs, but have come to the conclusion that this would be overkill, and instead use two Petzl locking oval krabs, as being the same shape as their mate in any direction keeps things tidy.

A further note on the attachment point is that I would get a secondary belay loop sewn on your harness for attaching the device (leaving the second one for daisy chains etc.). Further to this, I have also played around with creating a totally separate attachment system, designed to reduce the risk of an inverted fall. To do this I create a belay loop using 7 mm rope or 5.5 mm dyneema tied between my harness and my chest harness. This lifts the load point up above the waist and so helps to keep me upright in a fall. A secondary benefit is that the chest harness takes a higher percentage of the 'pull' on the device while leading, meaning your waist harness is not dragged down as much.

WARNING!
If you choose to make such a loop then make sure the length is set so that, in a fall, the device will not strike you in the face.

ROPES
You should treat your ropes as living things, always touching, moving and treating them with the utmost care and respect. These lengths of twisted nylon are the glue that sticks a climb together, the bridge that spans gravity and death, the means of your success or your retreat, but always your survival.

On a solo ascent your ropes will be pushed hard, leading, jumaring, rapping and hauling, so good quality cords are vital. At the same time you must take into account weight, bulk and their dynamic properties. On

08 EQUIPMENT

Aid climbing is a gear freak's dream, with tons and tons of fancy hard and software needed in order to pull off a climb. It's also very gear reliant, and not just the gear you plug into the rock, but also haul bags, bivy kit and fancy self-belay gadgets. If you're not a gear head, then big wall soloing is not the sport for you.

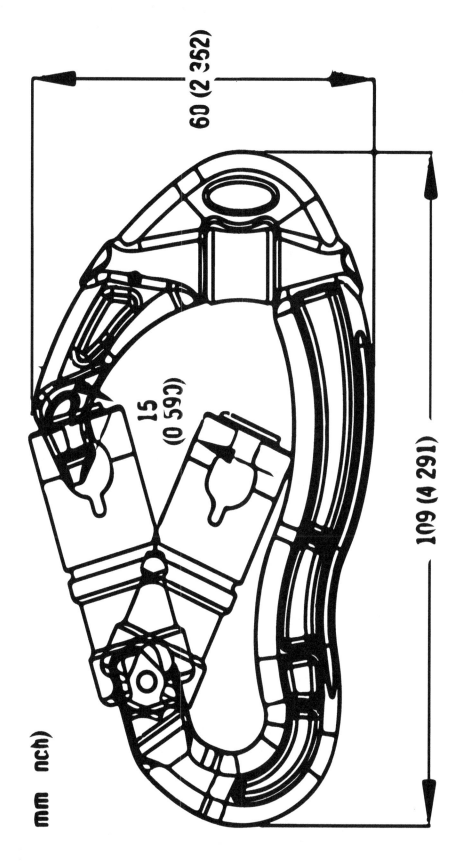

60 (2 352)

109 (4 291)

15
(0 590)

mm nch)

a remote wall weight can be a big factor, as a solo climber must carry all the weight on their shoulders, so may choose a 10 mm lead rope and a 9 mm static-haul line; a Yosemite climber might go for a 10.5 mm lead rope and a 10 mm static rope, as they only have a short approach.

LEAD ROPES

Diameter: I've used ropes from skinny 9.2 mm to chunky 11 mm, and each has its pros and cons. A skinny rope tends to wear faster and cause more concern when faced with lots of jumaring over edges, as well as when looking at falls on the very same edges. Their plus sides are low weight, bulk and a great dynamic properties (vital on walls with very low-strength protection (copperheads or birdbeaks)). Thick ropes on the other hand are seen as 'work' ropes, they are heavy, bulky and withstand much higher impact forces; the overall upside is, they last longer and provide more reassurance over edges and resilience to general wall abuse.

A problem worth noting with a thicker rope is that it won't move as smoothly through your self-belay device, which can have a bearing when free climbing, as the heavier the rope, the smaller the backup loop you need (a bigger backup loop allows you to climb further without resetting your backup knot). Of course between these two ropes you have the intermediate ropes, such as the 10.5 mm, which offer a compromise between these two extremes. Personally, I have found that ropes between 10 mm and 10.7 mm work fine on most walls.

Length: The minimum length for a lead rope should be 60 metres – the standard length these days. One of the best things about roped soloing is that there is zero drag as you are belaying from the leader's end (rather than from the belayer), and so travelling alone and through the protection line. A soloist could zigzag a rope all over a pitch and still have total freedom; this allows the leader to link pitches together with total ease. This can pay dividends as it is the setting up of the belay, rapping, cleaning and hauling, that eats up a lot of time, not the leading.

A great example of this was my attempt to solo the West Face of Leaning Tower in a day, when I linked the first four pitches with a single 80 metre rope! (NOTE that I free-aid soloed up the bolt ladder until the first non-bolted section to make it work). On many routes pitches can be linked with a 60 metre rope, but it's nice not to stress too much, so I would go for a 70 metre rope if possible (or even an 80 metre if you feel that you could link more pitches). On my attempt to solo the Eiger direct I actually used a 100 metre rope, which allowed me to find better belays, as well as reduce the time wasted finding them (on the Eiger it can take up to an hour to find and create a viable and safe solo belay). A longer rope also gives you spare rope if the ends become damaged.

Another reason for using a longer rope would be to have a single combined lead/haul line (so no knots joining the lead and haul line). This approach can work well on classic routes where pitches are shorter than 50 metres, as a single 100 metre rope would work, and could be lighter overall than two full length ropes (saying that, I've always signed up to the "where there's rope there's hope" school of rope length).

Colour: It may sound odd to mention rope colour, but a dark rope is harder to monitor from above compared to a white one, vital when it comes to avoiding cross clipping. Plus, a colourful rope is more cheerful.

HAUL LINE
The haul line is just as important as the lead line and is not only used to haul your bags, but also used to rap down at the end of a pitch and fix up the wall (before blasting off, or when climbing capsule style).

Static or dynamic?
A static rope is designed for much heavier abuse than a lead rope, its sheath is constructed to withstand jumars and pulleys, meaning it is perfect as a haul

line. The problem is that these ropes are designed for an industrial environment, a space with far more certainty than a big wall. On a wall your haul line may need to be pressed into service as a lead line if your lead rope becomes damaged, meaning a static rope will not do the job (well it can, but you must not fall!).

There is also the doomsday scenario that the lead line may be chopped in a fall, meaning the leader falls onto the haul line (this lead to the death of a climber on El Cap in 2013). By using a dynamic rope you increase redundancy in your system (you have two lead ropes), as well as safety (a fall onto a haul line would not be fatal). Another important factor is that when using the continuous loop method, you can pull up and begin clipping the haul line in an emergency (perhaps on very loose ground).

As for hauling on a dynamic rope my experience is that, once the rope is loaded, it actually makes very little difference if it's static or dynamic, as most of the stretch is ironed out by the weight of the bags. The main downside is that the sheath of a standard lead rope is not as robust as a static, so you need to choose your dynamic haul line well (like single ropes designed for professional use that feature a reinforced or thicker sheath). On the Reticent Wall I carried no set haul line, but three lead lines of 9.4 mm, 10 mm and 10.5 mm, and mixed and matched these ropes depending on the type of pitch (the 9.4 mm is very thin, but I used this on the A5 death crux pitch, as its low-impact force/high stretch gave me a higher degree of safety). I ended up splitting my load, so used one line for leading and the other two for hauling (by doing this I halved the overall abuse the ropes had to take).

Diameter: On an alpine wall, or when weight will be an issue, a 9 mm static rope works well and, although thin, this style of static rope still feels substantial and safe, even when rapping over roofs high above the talus. The norm for a static haul line would be 10 mm though, which provides a higher degree of strength, edge resistance and longevity when hauling super loads. For a dynamic haul line I think that unless it's a very small wall, or alpine, a 9 mm rope (or even 8.2 mm or 8.5 mm) is a bit too thin for heavy use, and I would go for a diameter between 9.5 mm and 10 mm.

One thing to note is that a static rope is in fact only semi static and is designed to take a fall without snapping (if it was as stiff as wire it would snap if loaded dynamically). This has been proved a few times by climbers dropping their haul bags by accident, the bags dropping 60 metres before coming to a jarring halt (three climbers died on the Nose due to their haul bag shock-loading their anchor in 1978, but this was down to a very poor 'death triangle' anchor and weak bolt).

Length: Your haul line should match your lead line in length and most will be 60 metres. Having a longer haul line of perhaps 70 or 80 metres can eliminate the need for a lower-out line (see below), as you can simply tie the bag in

short (so not at the end of the rope, but somewhere along it) to the haul line and leave what is left to lower the bag (I've used an 80 metre haul line on the Nose like this). A longer rope can also help if you decide to fix off a ledge, or can even be used to extend your lead line (once again, "where there's rope there's hope").

Cleaning cord: Traditionally when cleaning a pitch, the second will just lower out with the lead rope using various techniques (holding onto the rope below the lower jumar while releasing the cam, lowering with a GriGri, rapping from a piece), but for soloing it's worth employing a dedicated lower-out cord for major lower outs (generally from fixed gear), if you're stuffing the lead line away in a rope bag as you go. A 20 metre length of 6 mm cord (held in a small stuff sack) is used to lower out (6 mm cord is thin enough to slip through the eyes of pegs while your karabiner is still clipped in).

How to employ the lower-out

cord is covered in the Cleaning section.

Extra ropes: You may need to carry a lower-out line on routes that feature a great deal of traversing (if you can't tie your bags off short), and a 20 metre length of 6 mm cord tends to work fine. Stow it in a small stuff sack so it doesn't tangle, and when lowering, always use a monster munter hitch so you have plenty of control over it.

If you're climbing a route 'capsule' style, then you will need extra ropes to fix; I find 9mm static works well. The number of ropes you take depends on the terrain, but I find a 100 metre rope very useful, as this will often stretch over three pitches, or even four, and allow knot-free hauling when moving camps.

STANDARD EQUIPMENT

Big HMS lockers: It's a good idea to carry a few very large HMS auto lockers (Petzl, Yates, DMM) for use with haul bags, powerpoints and anywhere you will be clipping in multiple slings, krabs and ropes. At least one super large HMS (such as the Petzl William or DMM Boa) should be carried, as this will be vital for lowering bags in an emergency.

Mini lockers: On a normal team ascent you can make do with plain gates most of the time (clipping your cordelette into belays etc.), as there will always be someone there to keep an eye on them, but on solo climbs this is one 'i' that needs a dot. There are lots of really good tiny screwgates on the market these days, allowing 100% security in a host of situations, working better than larger, heavier, HMS krabs in many situations (GriGri krab, for use with prusik loops, connecting cord to belays). The weight difference is significant when you add up all the heavy-duty HMS krabs, so this is a good place to cut some of the load.

'Guide' belay device: You should never leave the belay without some way of rapping down a rope, and this device should have the extra functionality of acting as an auto-locking brake. This means you'll need some kind of 'guide'-style belay device such as the Petzl Reverso. The auto-locking mode can be used when you need a makeshift jumar (used for the feet with a mini ascender/prusik used above for the body), for easy hauling or as a backup self-belay device. A GriGri can come in very handy on a wall, but a Reverso-style device offers many added benefits, not least the ability to increase friction dramatically and in turn reduce heat build-up. To do this, add two (or even three) large HMS-style lockers to the clip-in biner (where the rope runs down and around), increasing friction dramatically – ideal when rapping with heavy loads.

It's very easy to drop a belay device, so firstly, always carry a spare in your grab bag, and secondly, have a systematic approach to clipping in and out of the belay device:

1. Your belay device should be a four part system, comprising a 'guide'-style device (Petzl Reverso) with two rope slots and a guide hole (the hole you

clip into the belay when using the device in auto-lock mode). The next two parts are two matched oval krabs with round bar sections (Petzl OK). The primary krab is the one used to clip to your belay loop (this will always be clipped through the device's retaining loop), while

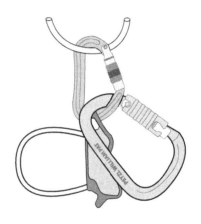

the second is used for auto-lock mode (clipped through guide hole, while the primary krab locks the rope), as well as a double up krab for increased friction on raps. The last piece of the system is a single strand lanyard tied with 3 mm cord (threading this through plastic tube will reduce tangles). This is tied from the belay device's guide hole to the primary krab.

2. The key to the system is that it is always racked through the guide hole, never through the retaining loop of the device. The primary krab is clipped/racked in the retaining loop, joined to the device also by the cord. The best method for not losing the device on connect/removal from the rope is to have it racked on your frontracking loop (you can clip it on your back, but this will increase the chance of a fumble). With the device still racked, take the rope(s) and insert them into the device and clip in the primary krab. You can now remove the device from the rack and clip onto your belay loop without fear of losing it. When removing, just reverse the process. Just make sure you don't end up rapping clipped onto your gear loop!

GriGri: Although a little bit of a luxury (and not something I would carry on lead), a GriGri can add a lot to your ability to stay safe and sorted on the wall. Here are a few reasons why it's worth having one:

1. It's a backup self-belay device if you lose your primary device.

2. It makes fixing down pitches on retreats a little easier.

3. It works well for hauling.

4. It can be used as a backup ascender (along with one jumar).

5. It's good for creating an quick and easy method of rope positioning when on ledges or bivys (you tie in the end of the rope, then clip in the GriGri and shorten your connection depending on how much slack you want).

6. Most useful of all is that the GriGri can be used as a 'movable knot' when jumaring/cleaning.

The GriGri is best left at the belay when leading and picked up and used once you return (if you don't mind the weight then you can simply carry it along with your guide belay device).

One modification (beyond those discussed above) is to attach a 3 mm loop of dyneema (you can thread it through plastic tubing to stiffen it up) through the clip in loop (you may need to cut away a small piece of plastic). This will allow you to take the GriGri on and off one handed (if injured), by allowing you to clip off the loop. When making a lanyard like this, make sure that there is no way the loop could interfere with the normal action of the GriGri.

Prusik loops: Always carry three 5 mm prusik loops (different colours), for self-rescue, rap anchors and for overcoming problems with other systems (untied, a prusik can form a mini releasable docking cord). Get cord that is 1.2 metres long (good for rap backup), 1.5 metres long (body pusik) and 2.5 metres long (foot prusik and self-rescue cord). Tie the two shorter cords with double fisherman's knots and the long cord with just a reef knot backup with double fisherman's knots (this will allow you to untie it easily if you need a single length of cord).

Jumars: When soloing you should always have some effective rope climbing tools on you at all times, either your handled jumars, or some micro ascenders (Petzl Tibloc, Kong Duck, Wild Country Ropeman), as these will be required if you're to deal with problems on lead.

Knife: I'm not a big fan of carrying a knife on my harness, but when you're soloing you need to be totally self-sufficient and you never know when one may come in handy. The small Petzl folding knives are very good value and work well but, like your nut tool, I'd add a short loop so as to reduce the chance of dropping it (this is also easier to clip into if you have an odd shaped racking krab).

Mini ascenders: Although they will add some extra weight, I would advise always having some small mechanical ascenders on your harness in case you lose an ascender, or forget to rap with them when cleaning. A Petzl Tibloc is only a little heavier than a prusik loop, but requires far less effort to use. If you choose to use Tiblocs, then make sure you practise with them beforehand and note that they need to be used with a round bar oval or HMS biner to function properly (D-shaped krabs will cause the Tiblocs to slip and damage the sheath ... and your underpants). If you carry a GriGri (even if it's left at the belay), then you can just take one Tibloc (although saying that, two aren't much heavier than one).

Petzl Micro Traxion: It may seem off having this pulley on your harness when you're already going to be using a full size pulley, but a Micro Traxion only weighs a little more than Tibloc and greatly increases your toolbox to deal with problems on the wall. It can be used as a highly effective jumar (the Traxion goes on waist and foot loop, the Tibloc goes above as foot loop attached to long prusik). Having a second pulley also allows you a backup close to hand, as well as the ability to 'up' your pulley system to a 2:1 or 3:1 at a moment's notice (carrying DMM Revolver krabs on long slings and shock absorbers gives you extra pulleys to use with your Micro and Pro Traxion).

Head torch: Although this isn't technical kit, find yourself alone in the dark without one and you'll understand its value! Always make sure you have a torch available when darkness is around the corner, as it's very easy to miscalculate the approach of darkness and end up far from the belay in the dark. On major routes I leave a small Petzl Tikka attached to my helmet at all time, tying it into one of the vents with 2 mm cord as a backup; I carry a secondary, more powerful, torch for when I don't have my helmet on, or for more difficult night-time climbing.

Shock absorbers: Roped soloing can slightly increase the shockloads applied to protection when climbing in some situations, and so having several shock-absorbing slings is a good move (Yates and Petzl make good ones). These are long slings, sewn together in a 'folded sandwich', which will sequentially pull apart under load, resulting in the force applied being spread over a longer period. Basically, the load applied must be taken by the protection, but if this load can be shared over a greater length of time, the peak force will be lower. You can further improve this by adding DMM Revolver biners to your shockers, as these reduce the friction on the piece, transferring it to the rope itself. Remember that the rope is the best way to absorb any force, and that the rope should ideally run directly from the belay to the piece being loaded (the rope from this piece to the falling climber is invariably straight), as this will allow the greatest stretch time (more time = lower weight/force on the protection). Just imagine pulling a 50 metre elastic band in a field, then doing the same in a wood with the band zigzagging between trees.

Gloves: If you trash your hands early on when climbing a wall then there is a good chance you'll not get to the top, so it's vital to look after them. No matter how tough they might appear to be, heavy hauling will see them blistered (blisters then burst and get infected), and leading will see your nails and cuticles ragged and painful. You need to keep your gloves on for most of the climb, only

removing them for harder free climbing (though it's worth noting that leather gloves actually work well for hand jams).

Fingerless leather gloves are the most common handwear for the wall (make sure they have a clip

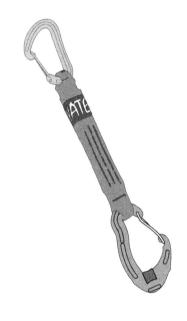

off loop), as they allow dexterity and adequate free-climbing flexibility (you can crimp and finger jam in them).

Personally I use full finger leather gloves these days

(Petzl work gloves), as I find that on a long solo, where you are basically climbing up and down three times, my fingertips always get trashed. By wearing full finger gloves my fingertips and nails stay pain free and I have fewer problems with infections. The downside is that my hands tend to get hotter ... worst of all, I end up with terrible tan lines.

Rope bags: These can either be dedicated rope bags (Fish make the best ones), or any large stuff sack (see Leading section for more info).

Survival gear: A soloist must be totally self-sufficient and able to deal with any and every situation. This includes being able to deal with storms, meaning you should have enough warm kit to survive any winter storm, as well as a bomb-proof fly/bivy bag and a warm sleeping bag (having a thin and a medium bag means you can tailor it to the temperature). The minimum kit would be a shell top and bottom, a fleece, a synthetic belay jacket, a hat, a balaclava and warm gloves. If there's the chance of a winter storm, then add in mitts, fleece pants and thermal underwear. Make sure everything is stowed in dry bags and always have a shell and fleece in your tag bag when bad weather is looming.

02

{ The Wall }

01 CONCEPTS

So now we get to the 'meat' of this book, how to actually get yourself from the bottom of a pitch to the top, from the first pitch to the last.

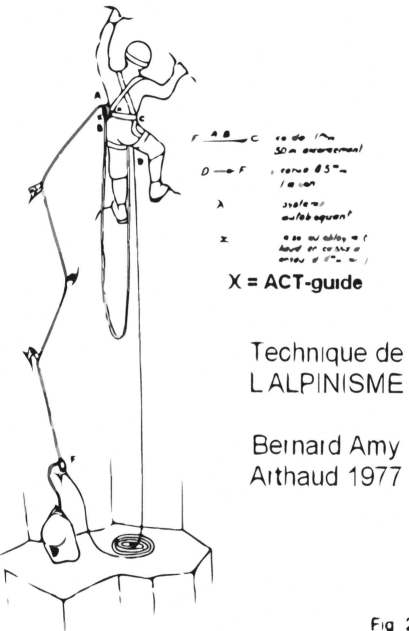

X = ACT-guide

Technique de
L ALPINISME

Bernard Amy
Arthaud 1977

Fig 253

The basic idea

Before we get into the nitty-gritty of rope soloing, let's look at how rope soloing works:

1. The climber arrives at the bottom of the climb and creates an anchor for both up and down forces.

2. They attach the rope to themselves and close to the anchor using either a knot (figure 8 or clove hitch), or a mechanical auto-locking belay device (Silent Partner or Soloist), and begin to climb, placing gear and clipping in as they go.

3. If they fall they will be caught by either their knot or mechanical device. If they are using a knot they must adjust it to give themselves some slack.

4. On reaching the top they create an anchor that is strong enough for both an upward and downward force.

5. They can now rap back down the rope, taking out their gear, or if the route is a traverse, rap

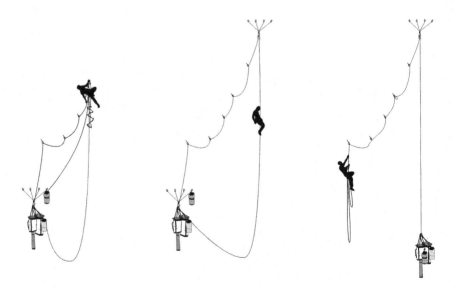

down a second free hanging rope (or haul line) attached to the belay.

6. On reaching the ground they strip the belay and climb back up the rope (via jumars or re-climbing) and begin again.

Using this system, the climber is safeguarded in case of a fall, with the drawback being that they must climb the pitch twice and also rap back down, so in effect, moving over the same ground three times. On a single pitch route this is fine, but on a very long route this requires a great deal of organisation, stamina and the ability to be self-aware (there is no one to check you but you).

Ok, so that's the basics. But before we get into the finer details, let's focus on some of the crucial concepts and components of the 'systems'.

02 FUNDAMENTALS

Before I continue onto the nuts and bolts and nitty gritty of big wall soloing, I'm going to cover a number of fundamental ideas you need to understand in order to make your systems work. These are often small details, things easily overlooked when learning how to rope solo, but they also tend to make or break a system, or even kill you if you ignore them completely!

The backup knot

The backup knot in any soloing system is your last line of defence, and although it may never be called on to hold a fall, if that day comes and you've skipped it, then you will probably slip off the rope and die.

The backup knot is used to create a solid non-moving connection to your lead rope and acts as your last line of defence in case your primary belay device fails. If you're soloing on knots then this chance is low, but even using a clove-hitch system, karabiners can become cross loaded and break, or gates can come undone. Even with an auto-feeding device like a GriGri, your backup may well end up being loaded, as all these devices are open to failure.

Smooth sailing: A secondary reason for the backup knot, and perhaps the most important for the smooth running of your systems, is that the loop the backup knot creates (between the knot and the device) allows your rope to feed smoothly through your auto-belay device. Imagine you begin at the belay with your rope stacked in its bag, fed through the device but with no backup knot. As you climb, the rope (attached to the belay at one end, which we'll called the 'live' rope) will move through your device smoothly, but as you get higher your movement is pulling the rope through the device. Eventually the weight of the live rope will be great enough for the live side of the rope to pull the dead side through, hence the use of rope holders (see diagram).

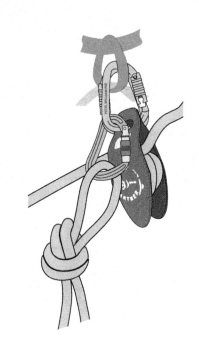

As you get higher the weight of the dead rope, as well as the drag on the live rope, will begin to tip the balance in favour of the dead rope. When it does this the rope will begin to 'snatch' on the device, a common problem when learning to solo. Now if you pull up several metres of slack in the dead rope, and tie in with a backup knot, the weight of most of the dead rope is apportioned to you, not the device, and the rope will run smoothly again.

The size of this loop depends on the weight and diameter of the rope, how it interacts with the design of the device and the amount of protection clipped. When aiding I will give myself a loop of around 10 metres, as this means I can move for a while without having to worry about it; if I'm free climbing, I'll try and make it a little longer.

The knot: The backup knot can be any of your choosing as long as it's strong and solid. For general use a figure 8 works fine, clipped into a small locker on your belay loop. For speed you can use a clove hitch, as this can be released one handed. When you're getting close to the end of your backup you should notice the loop getting short and so you should try to create a new loop, tie a knot and clip in the new one before unclipping the old one. Invariably you always end up having the backup come tight when you least want it, such as mantling onto a ledge! For this reason, always check and extend it before any free climbing.

Micro Traxion system

Speed climbers have begun feeding their dead rope through a Micro Traxion so they can gain slack instantly (no knot to unclip or untie), making free climbing much easier. Adding a toothed jumer on the dead side of the rope could be very hazzerdous if your belay device was to fail, so a back up knot should still be employed. The Traxion is not load baring so can be clipped onto a racking loop. *This is a very advanced and dangerous technque so please take the time to understand its dangers.*

Dead rope/live rope

This is a vital concept for rope soloing systems as it allows you to understand what can be clipped and how to overcome potential errors in your system. To do this we divide the rope between the live rope and the dead rope. The basic principle is: The live rope is the rope between the anchor and your belay device. As you climb the length of live rope increases.

The dead rope lives in its rope bag at the belay and is attached to nothing but you (via your device and backup knot). Once the dead rope passes through your belay device it becomes live rope. Dead rope allows you to ascend and once you have run out of it (where it has become live rope), you can go no further.

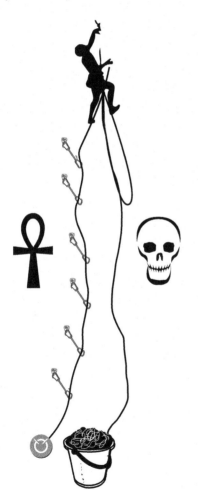

Try and visualise this idea of the live and dead rope when setting up your systems and when leading, as it can help to avoid mistakes.

Bagging

To get your system to work you need to bag your lead and haul lines. A rope bag is simply a way of storing a rope so that it will pay out remotely without snags and tangles, this is vital when you have no belayer to sort out such problems. Bags are set at belays with the rope carefully fed, so that it will feed out perfectly, and vary from custom-made Cordura bags designed for soloing walls to a simple Ikea carrier bag.

Your rope bags will be both your best and worst friend on the wall, creating lots of seemingly endless work (stuffing rope bags can make you feel like Sisyphus!), but like your rope, you need to give them great respect and care (otherwise they won't care for you).

You essentially need a bag that is big enough to hold one full size rope with a little space left over, it shouldn't be too narrow or too wide, and should have at least one clip loop to attach it to the belay (or better still, two attachments, so the bag can be held open when stuffing). On most walls you will need two rope bags (one for the lead line and one for the haul line), but three will be needed if doing a double haul. On alpine or speed ascents you can keep things simpler by just using your rucksack as a rope bag (this only works when using one rope), or even a hole dug in the snow, but for anything big I would always take rope bags.

Rope bags serve a secondary purpose on bivys where they make very good stuff sacks to hold kit when emptying haul bags (ropes will need to be coiled when not stuffed into bags).

Rope bag tech

When stowing a rope in a bag you need to give it the same care and attention as if you were packing a parachute. As with a parachute, when you pull you want the correct outcome! Sloppy rope stuffing

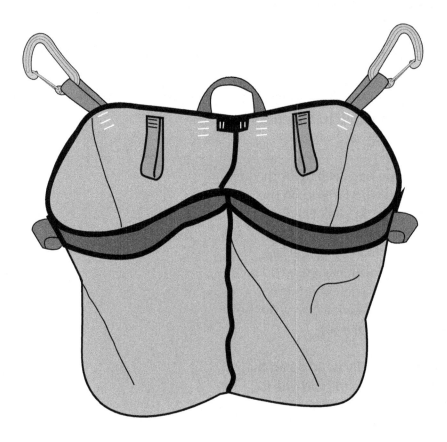

will see you come to a halt half way up a pitch and will lead to a great deal of wasted time and frustration, so get it right!

To stow a rope correctly you must avoid just grabbing handfuls of rope and stuffing it in as if you were stuffing a turkey. No! You must slowly feed in the rope as if icing a cake, one strand feeding over another and another. Smoothly and carefully in = smoothly and perfectly out.

The two best techniques involve 'pulling' the rope down into the bag, rather than trying to feed it in, while holding the rope's weight. To do this you need to first run the rope through a karabiner set above the bag (using this as a pulley), pulling the rope down with both hands and feeding it into the bag. An improved method is to use a small locking pulley like a Micro Traction, as this will also hold the weight of the rope as it is fed in.

Again, whenever you stick your rope into a rope bag, imagine you are packing a parachute.

03 THE BELAY

The big wall solo belay can range from the super simple: just two solid 10 mm bolts, to the highly complex: a mix of cams, pegs and nuts working in multiple directions and all equalised to a single point. Whatever type of belay you are forced to build, it must provide total security, as the forces that might be applied can be much higher than with a partner. All big wall belays must be able to withstand standard loads as well as the huge loads created by hauling (over twice the total weight of your bags), as well as a potential direct falls onto the belay (factor 2).

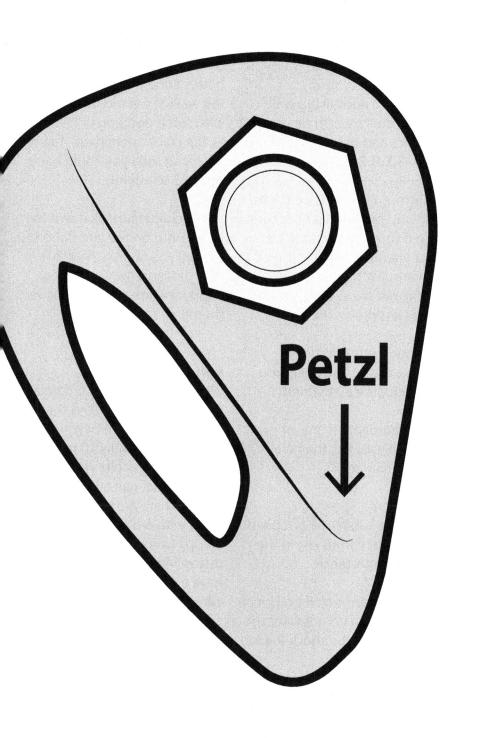

Having climbed some walls already means you will understand normal big wall belays, but it's worth going back to basics and trying to conform to the **S.E.R.E.N.E** standard:

• **S** (Strong): The belay must be solid and provide 100% security even if some of its component parts are marginal (it is the 'powerpoint' that must be strong, not necessarily the 20 pieces it is drawn from!);

• **E** (Equalised): In order to achieve this strong belay you must equalise everything;

• **R** (Redundant): If one, or even several pieces fail, the belay must remain solid;

• **E** (Efficient): Speed is important, especially on speed ascents, but comes last in the order of importance;

• **NE** (No Extension): If one piece should fail you do not want the whole belay to be shock-loaded.

I've experienced a whole gamut of belays, from A6 belays made from birdbeaks and micro nuts on poor limestone, expanding belays (where cams shifted once the weight came onto them, with some popping or inverting as the crack opened up), to bolt belays so solid you could hang the QE2 off them!

I've decided to break down the belays into bolted and unbolted, as how you approach each is very different (as well as how happy you are climbing above them!).

Bolted belays

When I talk about bolted belays I'm talking about belays that have bolts that are beyond question, generally 10 mm stainless steel bolts with hangers that can take well over 30 kN. There are belays out there with old skinny bolts and crappy Leeper hangers, or self drives with alloy hangers that have corroded to the point where they have the strength of a cream cracker, but for these we would treat them as part of the secondary category. On El Cap, by and large, every bolt you come across will be a new one, and there will often be several to choose from.

Spartan belay:
If we accept that any single bolt in our belay could technically be strong enough to form our belay (most bolts will hold more than 2,500 kg), then we don't need to equalise the belay, but only connect the bolts somehow for redundancy; this way we save a great deal of time and equipment, and have a higher belay point, crucial for hauling (of course we break the S.E.R.E.N.E Redundancy rule, however, these rules were intended for trad belays, so we have slowly re-tuned the S.E.R.E.N.E rules when it comes to well-bolted routes).

For this set up, all you require is two micro lockers and a large HMS auto locker (ideally auto lockers, but a screwgate is fine), and your rope; that's it, no cordelette or slings are needed. You can carry these three krabs neatly on the back of your harness (clip both small lockers into the big one).

Here is how it would work with a standard rope soloing set up:
1. You arrive at bolted belay and clip in with both daisy chains

(one on each bolt).

2. You clip one small locker onto each bolt, clipping the large HMS

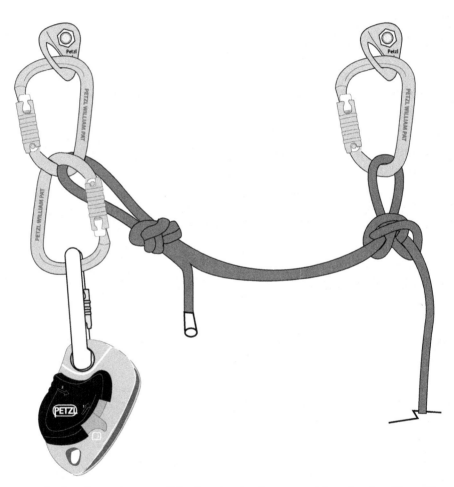

auto locker into the small locker in the best position for hauling (if they are both the same then clip to the right bolt if right handed and vice versa).

3. Take the end of the lead line, tie a figure 8 and clip this into the single small locker, then tie an alpine butterfly and clip this into the locker paired with the HMS (a butterfly knot is used as you will be jugging up on this rope, and so will be easier to untie).

4. The HMS is your powerpoint and into this will be clipped your hauler, the high positioning of the hauler direct to the bolt rather than at the bottom of a cordelette tends to aid hauling.

5. Once set up, you will take the end of the haul line and take the haul line locker (the locker attaching the haul line to your rear haul loop) and clip it into the empty locker, then tie an alpine butterfly and clip this into the powerpoint. You could just clip the haul line into the powerpoint, but this way you achieve some redundancy when rapping down the haul line.

6. After you've rapped the haul line and cleaned the pitch, you will haul the bag up, hanging it from the powerpoint via its docking cord.
The main thing to remember is that the end of the lead line (the end furthest from the belay), is going to be used to form the new belay when you arrive, an effect best visualised as leapfrogging the rope up the wall (the end you untie below on the last belay will be tied again into the next belay above).

If you're running a continuous loop system you will need to untie the ends.

Traditional belay: This would be the 'go to' belay for anyone wanting to do it the standard way, conforming to S.E.R.E.N.E and ticking all the safety boxes. To do this you clip either plain gate or mini lockers to the bolts (two bolts are fine, but three may make your mum happier); I tend to go with a mix, always having one micro locker.

Here, you equalise everything to a single point, the powerpoint, using either:

• Two 60 cm slings clipped off to one bolt each (no need to equalise, plus no knots to untie);

• One long 120 cm sling clipped to two bolts, with a sliding X (you can leave this set up as a pre-build belay rig);

• Cordelette. You can use this to equalise two or three bolts, it can also come in handy if you have a mix of bolts and trad gear, but generally on bolted belays it's slower than the above;

• 'Fancy-pants' slings. You can buy numerous fancy equalising slings, designed by people who do more climbing in their head than on the crag, and bought by people unjustifiably paranoid. Keep it simple, as the above systems are much more flexible and have multiple uses (for

example, a cordelette can come in very handy when setting up releasable attachment points).

Belay powerpoint: Everything is equalised down to the powerpoint, which is best created using the strongest forged HMS you can find (the biggest HMS krabs are vital when lowering bags using a monster munter). Nothing should be clipped directly into this apart from other krabs, so that the powerpoint never needs to be opened when loaded. Instead, you clip in your lead rope, haul line, hauler etc.

Non-bolted belays
On a non-bolted belay you need to think about S.E.R.E.N.E in a different way, in fact you just need add W.U.D at the end (however, S.E.R.E.N.E.W.U.D doesn't roll off the tongue); these letters standing for 'Works Upside-Down'. On a normal trad belay, we're told we must have pieces that work with an upward pull, but in fact we tend not to bother, believing that the weight of a belayer is enough to stop the belay from being yanked up and out (I've heard of belays ripping when the leader has fallen directly onto the belay (factor 2), but never in a standard fall onto a runner above. On a solo wall the chances of an upward pull versus a downward pull are reversed, as any fall is hopefully going to be upward. At the same time, the belay must withstand the huge forces of big wall climbing, which all adds up, thus having to have really bomber belays.

One thing to remember is that cams and pegs tend to work in any direction, so if you have a couple of good cams and a peg, then you're sorted in any direction, and the traditional three-piece belay should be OK. If you can't place cams and have to rely on nuts, then these tend to only work in one direct of pull, meaning you will need to place upward pulling nuts as well.

The poorer the rock and the more sparse the placements, the further out you will need to hunt for good gear, maybe even climbing a little way up the next pitch. On such routes I would take four cordelettes, perhaps using two on one belay (practise using a cordelette both as a round sling and untied to form a snake sling), and use the standard equalised belay, employing every technique I could to reduce the force on the belay. You may even be forced to employ the rope as well.

On such routes you may find that your rack gets gobbled up, so take a third more gear to deal with this problem; on the hardest routes taking a longer rope (70, 80 or 100 metres) can allow you to limit the number of poor belays you need to deal with.

The bottom line is never accept a poor belay when soloing, even if it means retreating.
Other important aspects of the belay matrix

Dynamic haul bag belay: On hard aid it's very important that you achieve as dynamic a belay as possible, as the greater the amount of time allowed to absorb any force, the lower the peak force. Your lead rope has the greatest capacity to absorb this force (the thinner it is, the longer it stretches, therefore the more time to absorb the force), but with some forethought when setting a belay, you can use the belay itself to decrease the peak force dramatically. The one object that is able to move (and is also the one object heavy enough to counter your body weight), is your haul bag. By integrating your bag into the belay matrix you can dramatically reduce the peak forces involved in a fall.

The trick is to hang the haul bag lower than normal, so that the bag can be lifted a longer distance, basically like a counterweight. Again the thing to remember is that the peak force is calculated as force divided by time, and so a heavy bag being lifted up will absorb a great deal of force. When hauling normally you would haul the bag up until it is close to the powerpoint, but on a solo where low forces are vital you would tie it off via its docking cord, perhaps a metre or more lower. If you want to

gain access to the bag when you arrive you can always haul haul, then just drop it down again to lead (always have the haul line clipped in as a backup to the bag's docking cord).

Once the bag is a metre below the belay you would run the lead line from the belay (the belay is still the primary attachment point), down to the bags and clipped in with an alpine butterfly to the hanging point (probably the swivel) with

NOTE: DIAGRAM MISSING
HAUL LINE BACK-UP FOR
CLARITY

a locking krab.

It is for this reason that I would recommend a dynamic 8 mm to 9 mm docking cord of at least 6.5 metres (the docking cord is doubled, so this will give you about 3 metres of play).

You can further increase the shock absorbance of the belay by using the following extra components.

• Shock-absorbing sling: This is a simple one, with the lead line being clipped into a ripper sling clipped off to the bag. In a fall directly onto the belay or a hard fall onto protection the ripper sling would engage and reduce the peak force on either the top runner or the belay itself. In a lead fall that is not onto the belay you tend not to create enough force to cause the

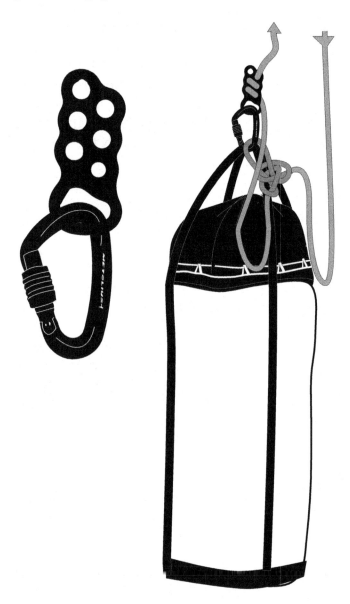

sling's stitching to rip. This sling would be attached to the haul bags with a locker and the rope would be attached to the other end with a locker.

• Kong KISA Shock Absorber: This is a small alloy plate full of holes, looking a little like a belay device. The rope is threaded through the holes in order to create friction (you can adjust the friction by how many holes you thread). As with the ripper sling this would be attached at the haul bag, with the lead rope either passing through it (slow to set up), or attached by a secondary rope.

Belay seat: On a steep wall not being able to take the weight of either your feet or your harness can be very draining, especially if the route is very long. Having a belay seat of some kind, either a soft one made from fabric (Yates or Fish), a solid seat (Petzl or Black Diamond), or even a hammock, can really help to reduce both the mental and physical strain of being on the wall.

Racking daisy: Stringing a daisy chain between two pieces of gear is a great way to sort it out, clipping it in and out of the pockets. The best thing about this system is that it eliminates the possibility of one end becoming unclipped and all the gear sliding off into the void! I will often stow my main gear on a daisy chain in my tag back, with less useful gear placed in the bottom in a stuff sack (pegs, spare hooks, heads, bolt kit).

04 LEAD SYSTEMS

I'm going to set out all the systems used for rope soloing, beginning with the basic systems, and working up to the more complex ones. I would recommend that everyone starts with the basics, practice them until they are understood, then move on to the next technique.

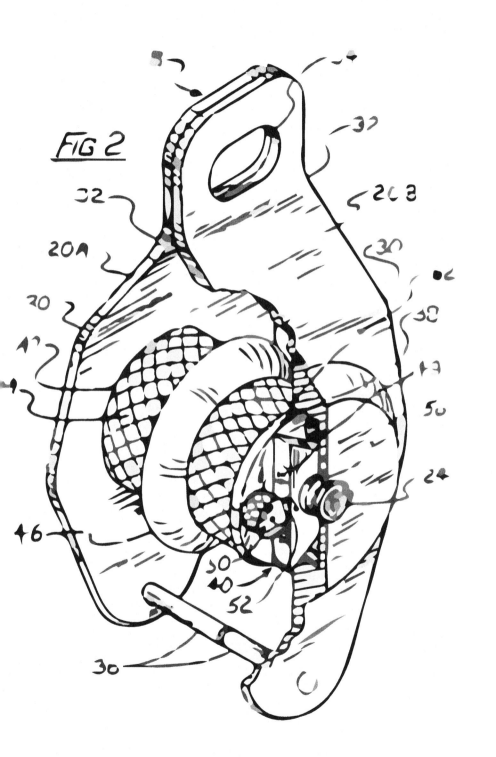

FIG 2

Clove hitch

I'm going to begin by describing
a pure rope solo system, with
no hauling or fancy tricks, as
this is the system you will use
when training. Once mastered,
you can add hauling, cleaning
and advanced variations as your
skills increase.

Scenario: Before you is a short
crag, only 20 metres high, the
route you want to climb is well
within your grade. There is a
two bolt belay anchor at ground
level and bolts at the top, with
a bolt every metre up the climb.
You are going to rope solo this
short route to test the systems,
not yourself (that will come
later).

Nuts and bolts: In terms of
equipment, you have a bunch
of quick draws, several locking
krabs, a 10 mm rope and a large
stuff sack to use as a rope bag.

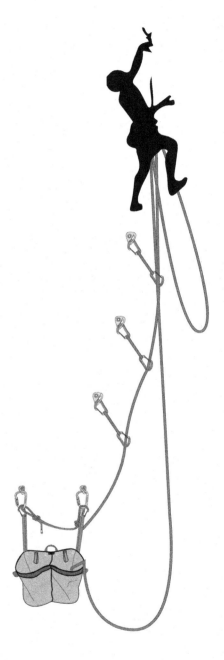

STEP BY STEP

1. You tie a figure 8 into the very end of the rope and clip this into the first belay bolt, then an alpine butterfly a little way higher, and clip this into the second bolt (both with locking krabs), creating an equalised belay. By removing slings from the system you are reducing the number of links in your safety chain and making it marginally more dynamic (dyneema slings are static). This will be the start of your live rope (try and imagine it 'plugged' into the mountain).

2. You now take the other end of your rope, the dead end (not plugged into anything), and begin to feed it onto the rope bag until all the rope is fed in.

3. Clip a locking krab to your belay loop, take some rope, and clip it into to the krab with a clove hitch. This will be your primary selfbelay point, with the knot being loosened and re-tied as you climb (as it's a clove hitch, you will never need to untie it, just loosen and reset).

4. You are now stood with the the dead rope on one side feeding out of the rope bag and up to your clove hitch, and the live rope leading from the clove hitch to the belay.

5. Now tie a backup knot by taking several metres of dead rope and tie a figure 8, clip this in with a small locker to your belay loop.

6. Giving yourself three metres of slack on your live rope by paying rope through your clove hitch, you can now climb up three metres, clipping the live rope into the protection as you go.

7. After three metres the live rope begins to get tight and the clove hitch begins to cinch down on the krab. You stand in balance and with one hand you pay out three more metres of rope (being careful not to place your finger inside the knot, but pinching it instead, in case you fall and the knot traps your fingers).

8. Having slack on your live rope you move up three more metres.

9. At this point your backup knot begins to get tight, so you stand in balance and pull up several metres of dead rope, tie a figure 8, and clip this into the small backup locker and switch out the original knot and untie it.

10. You climb on, moving the live rope through the clove hitch every three metres, the backup knot every ten metres.

11. Without warning you suddenly slip off, and fall one metre onto the bolt below. The clove hitch cinches down tight as the weight comes onto the live rope and you stop dead. Checking yourself, you climb back up and continue on (after a little battle undoing the clove hitch).

12. You reach the top of the route!

Auto belay variation

1. You return to the bottom and pull your rope, and stack the lead rope into its rope bag.

2. Instead of tying in with a clove hitch, this time you attach a Rock Exotica Silent partner using two lockers.

3. Now you tie a backup as you did in the basic system.

4. This time as you climb there is no need to keep fiddling with knots, as the device just feeds the rope out. You no longer feel quite so aware that you are rope soloing and feel you could probably climb at the limit of your grade.

5. After several metres your backup knot goes tight and you re-tie it as before, doing this a few times until you reach the top.

6. What you notice is that the climbing is much easier, as you don't need to nurse the knot all the time.

7. This time when you reach the top, you decide to rap down the rope in order to get the gear out, which you do with ease as the rope is running straight down. You tie off the rope to the top anchor and rap down.

8. Once at the bottom you untie the bottom belay and jumar back up the lead rope, pulling the rope up once you're at the top.

9. So far so easy.

Basic rope solo and haul system

This time we're going to add a bit more complexity to the system so as to allow you to climb multi-pitch routes, as well as haul.

Scenario: This time you have chosen to climb a five pitch route, again with bolt belays every forty metres and bolts every metre. You will also be hauling a small haul bag with tea and sandwiches in it.

Nuts and bolts: You have the same rack and rope setup as before, but now you have a 9 mm static rope and a second rope bag. You also have two long slings to create belays (each with two small lockers and a large high strength HMS krab to create a powerpoint), and a Petzl Micro Traxion.

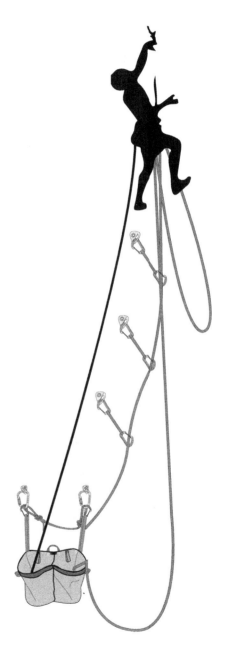

STEP BY STEP

1. As before, you set up a belay with your lead line, tying it to the bolts with two krabs, you stuff the rope into the rope bag and attach your Silent Partner and backup knot.

2. You now clip the haul line to the belay with a locking krab and begin feeding the rope into the rope bag (belay end first). A good way to speed this up is to run the rope through a mini locking pulley such as a Petzl Micro Traxion. When the rope is stacked away you will have one end free on the top. Tie a figure 8 and clip this to the back of your harness.

3. You begin climbing as before and as you do, the dead end of the lead rope feeds out of the rope bag and the haul line feeds out of the other rope bag. You stop every so often to re-tie your backup knot, but now you have a little more understanding about the length needed for the rope to run smoothly, you make the loops a little bigger, and so climb faster.

4. You reach the next belay station and set it up with your slings and krabs (creating a powerpoint) and pull up the dead end of the lead line first, clipping this to the powerpoint. You have a 60 metre rope, but the pitch is only 40 metres high, meaning you now have 20 metres of dead rope between your Silent Partner and the belay. You know you want to jumar back up this rope and so need it tight to the belay; you could, perhaps, pull this slack through once you get to the bottom belay, but this runs the risk of the rope hanging up (you could fall if you don't have that 20 metres pulled through). Instead you simply tie an alpine butterfly knot in the lead rope a metre from your device and clip this into the belay via a second locking karabiner (this is your 'tie-off' knot). This means you have very little slack in the system and you can jumar up easily (note: you should not pull the live rope tight, as this might make cleaning the bottom belay much harder).

5. Remember: when moving up a wall via multiple belays, the dead end becomes the live end at each pitch (and vice versa).

6. The lead rope sorted, you now unclip your haul line from the back of your harness (don't drop it!) and clip the end directly into a bolt. By doing this you can easily locate it and clip it to your harness once the rope is stacked and stored before the next pitch, plus it gives some redundancy. You now pull up approximately two metres of haul line (this will be used to do your initial hauling) and clip the haul line into the Petzl Micro Traxion (you can back this up by tying a figure 8 or alpine butterfly and clipping that just after the hauler), clip this into the powerpoint (note: you do not need to pull all the haul line tight to the belay, as you will shorten the haul line at the far end).

7. You attach your belay device to the haul line (making sure you have your jumars so you can re-climb the pitch) and then unclip from the Silent Partner.

8. You rap the haul line and reach the belay below (have a daisy chain and aider ready to clip in).

9. You secure yourself with both aiders (never trust a single point) and unclip from the haul line.

10. You now pull the haul line tight, and tie an alpine butterfly, clip it to your haul bag, and lower out the bag from the belay, ready to be hauled from above once you are back at the belay.

11. You take apart the belay and tie into the end of the lead line (as a backup). Now you begin to climb the rope, cleaning the protection a you go (you can tie backup knots as you go, or use a GriGri as a running knot).

12. Once you reach the belay you take the bottom end of the rope (which you clipped onto your harness as a backup at the bottom) and begin to stack it back into the rope bag, removing the 'tie-off knot' as you go, stopping when you only have a small two metre loop left (this is the rope you will attach your soloing device to).

13. Now you begin to bring up the haul bag, pulling the haul line into the haul-line rope bag as you go (this way, the line is stowed and ready for the next pitch, as well as out of harm's way).

14. With the bag up, you remove the Micro Traxion and clip it onto your harness, then unclip the haul-line krab and clip this to your harness also.

15. Now attach your soloing device, tie your backup knot and clip it in and double check everything is going to run smoothly.

16. Begin climbing, repeating as you go.

Continuous loop method
The above method is quite simple once you understand it and is easy to repeat, working well on most walls. The problem with it is that, at the end of a pitch, you can have quite a lot of weight on you (live and dead rope, plus haul line), which can be wearing, but worst of all you forced to carry your entire rack.

On a standard route this isn't too much of a problem and having a full set of cams, nuts and quickdraws is something most climbers can take. The problem comes on harder routes where you have no idea what you may need, where you may have pegs, copperheads, triples or even quads of cams, not to mention ice tools and crampons (in some cases). What if the pitch takes you six hours or more? Are you going to take food and water on your harness as well?

The continuous loop method is designed to both simplify true process, reduce the weight on your harness, and allow the tagging of gear. Before I talk about the tagging method, I'll just run through a non-tagging scenario.

Continuous loop (non-tagging)
We're back at our multi-pitch crag, ready to try a new technique, with the same gear as before (lead line/haul line, rope bags etc.).

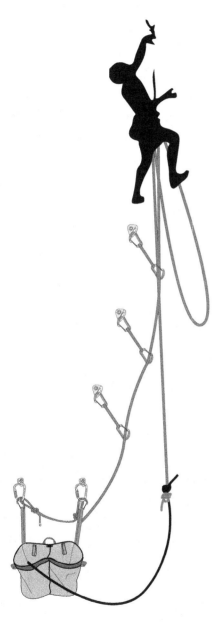

STEP BY STEP

1. You set up your belay as before and stack your lead rope in the rope bag, only this time you leave the dead end sticking out of the rope bag. Now you stack your haul line with the far end sticking out. Instead of attaching the haul line to the back of your harness, you tie the end of it to the dead end of the lead line, with a double fisherman's knot (you can use any knot really, but low profile is good).

2. You attach your Silent Partner as before, with backup knot etc., and begin climbing. You are using a 60 metre rope and now you don't have to worry about three strands of rope below you, just two (live and dead rope). At 30 metres (less as you're using a backup knot, which uses up quite a bit of rope), the dead end of the rope leaves the rope bag and begins to pull up the end of the haul line (where they are tied).

3. At the belay you untie both ropes, setting up the lead and haul line as normal. You stick the haul line through the hauler and set it up as before.

4. You rap and clean the pitch, and re-stack all ropes in their rope bags; tie the dead end of the lead line to the end of the haul line and begin again.

Continuous loop (with tagging)

The knot that joins the two ropes can be used as a connection point where you can attach a tag bag, allowing you to pull up the bag, either when you need it, or when you reach the halfway point on your lead line (each time you reach half way on the rope you have, you will need to pull up the tag bag).

Before we get into this let's look at the tag bag ...

Tag bag: It could be possible to just hang all your rack from the rope, but there is a good chance it would jam or hang up on the belay while being pulled up, so instead we use a tag bag. The tag bag is a medium sized haul bag, big enough to take both the rack and 30 metres of lead line (I use a small haul bag). Instead of being clipped into the rope, the tag bag is suspended from a fifi hook (attached via a locking oval) with a sturdy prusik loop (threaded through the lifting hole in the fifi) being used to prusik it close to the connection point between the ropes.

Set-up: Before you set off, you have your continuous loop system all set up, only this time you attach the tag bag via its prusik loop at the joint knot, then hang the tag bag from a bolt. You need to pay close attention at this point that both the lead and haul line still feed out of their bags smoothly and will not become fouled or tangled up by anything (lead line running around a haul bag strap for example). As the dead end of the lead line comes out of its rope bag, it should pull directly onto the fifi. Once this happens you can pull up the tag bag and this will pull up the haul line. Most times you will only need to pull up the tag rack after half a rope length, as you should be able to see what you need. At this halfway mark you will pull up the tag bag (it should be light enough for you to just hand over hand it), and once up, hang the fifi off the gear you're on (or the gear below). You will now have your tag bag with a 30 metre loop of lead line. At this point begin stuffing the rope back into the stuff sack inside the tag bag (dead end goes in first).

One advantage of this system is that once hung, the tag bag takes the weight of the haul line,

and if connecting the rope to protection to stop back-slipping, you can end up with no weight on you at all, which can be great on long hard pitches.

Once you've pulled the bag up half way, you will need to pull it up again within 15 metres (30 metre loop divided by two), then 7 metres, then 3, by which point you will be at the belay.

Notes about continuous tagging:

If you use a dynamic haul line in your continuous loop, this allows you to switch from the lead line to the haul line in an emergency. If your lead line is damaged or cut, or you're faced with an area where the rock is really worrying you (you're afraid your lead line may be cut), then you can use the haul line instead, or use both. To do this you would:

1. Make an intermediate mini belay from two or three runners.

2. Pull up the tag bag and attach it directly to this belay, removing it from the continuous loop.

3. Remove any knots and prusiks from the rope.

4. Make sure you take any rack you need from the tag bag as you will not be able to get it once you've start climbing.

5. Clip both the haul line and lead line sides of the loop into the mini belay.

6. Pull all the haul line up so that both ends (haul and lead line) are tight to the belay.

7. Starting at the joining point of the loop, feed this into the rope bag inside the tag bag.

8. Once stacked away, use some form of self-belay on the haul line as well as the lead line (probably a clove hitch).

9. Climb clipping both ropes or place one rope off to the side.

10. Once through the

ROPE BAG

RACK BAG

STORM GEAR

dangerous section you can switch back to just the lead line (or continue with both).

11. When you rap the haul line, make sure you unclip it from all protection.

A soloist's pitch, is one that's led, cleaned and hauled, and so half a pitch is one that's just lead, meaning that you clean and haul the pitch the following morning. This approach works on many levels. Firstly, it's vital to set a pace that's sustainable and doesn't leave you exposed by exhaustion. Soloing requires sound judgment and being strung out, especially in the dark, is a sure-fire way to get into trouble. So knowing your limits and only climbing what you can comfortably manage is the way to go. Keep a good safety margin by starting in the light and finishing before it gets dark. Darkness adds a whole new set of problems for the soloist and is best avoided unless you plan on setting speed records.

Having a rope fixed on the pitch above gives an extra level of safety, as your belay is backed up by the belay above.

The first thing I do is stack my ropes, which being tired the night before, I just left looped on the belay. I set both rope bags and carefully feed both the haul and lead lines into their bags (the free end goes in first on lead line and last on the haul line). Once this is done I check that my lead rope is attached to the powerpoint of the belay correctly and backed up directly to a bolt. With my haul bag hanging from the powerpoint I know that a pull on the lead line will lift up the bag and help provide a soft fall.

The Slippery Hitch
The slippery hitch is well worth learning, as it can add an extra layer of security when tagging your bag, plus it's a neat trick that may prove handy some other time. When tagging, the rope from the bag is fed from its connection to the bag, up past the fifi, and looped several times through the krab the bag is hanging from. This is done by passing a bite of rope through a seperate karabiner, then pass a bite through this loop, and again and again, creating a daisy chain of loops. Practice this knot as much as you can, and you'll see if the bag falls off the anchor the hitch locks off, and yet can be untied by pulling the knot from above.

When using a slippery hitch pay close attention to where the loop lays, and that it won't tangle or catch on any other part of the system.

Slippery Hitc

05 ERRORS

Knowing what to do, and why you do it is vitally important when there is only you to check yourself. Yet no matter how good you are, there will be mistakes, especially when you're tired or pushing yourself hard. Here I've listed the major errors you may encounter on a solo ascent, how to avoid them and what to do if you didn't.

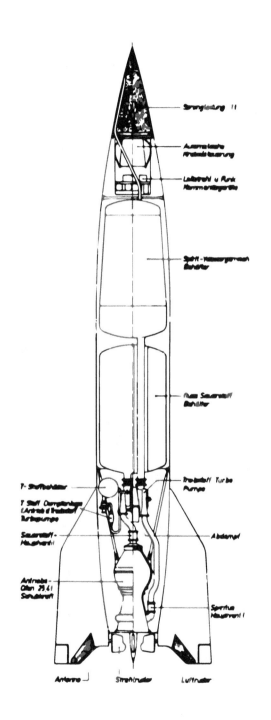

Sprengladung 11

Automatische
Kreiselsteuerung

Leitstrahl u. Funk
Kommandogeräte

Stoff-Wassergemisch
Behälter

Fluss Sauerstoff
Behälter

T-Stoffbehälter

T Stoff Dampferzeuger
(Antrieb d Treibstoff
Turbopumpe)

Sauerstoff-
Hauptventil

Antriebs-
Ofen 29,6t
Schubkraft

Treibstoff Turbo
Pumpe

Abdampf

Spiritus
Hauptventil

Antenne   Strahlruder   Luftruder

BACK-SLIPPING

Error: The weight of the lead rope below the leader clipped into the gear causes the rope to begin feeding in reverse back through the device.

One vital but often overlooked item of soloing equipment is the rope stopper (or stoppers, as more than one may be required). These are basically light duty prusiks designed to take the weight of the rope below you so that: (a) the weight of the down rope does not pull the up rope through the belay device in reverse; and (b) by taking the weight off the rope you allow your self-belay device to run smoothly.

Consider this scenario: You lead a straight up pitch for 20 metres, having a backup loop (the loop between your backup knot and your device). Without warning the rope begins to slip backwards through your belay device, only stopping when it comes tight on the knot. What has happened is that the weight of the down rope has become greater than the up rope,

meaning it is dragged down. In most cases this is just annoying, but it could be more serious if you were in the middle of free climbing and all of a sudden the rope went whizzing back through your device.

Avoiding the problem: By attaching a small prusik loop to a piece of protection and onto the rope, this can take the weight off the rope and eliminate the problem.

A few things to consider about your rope stopper is its strength and stretch. Strength is not that important, in fact I think that having a high strength prusik could be a hinderance, as you can end up just jumaring up on a single piece of gear (backed up to the belay) if you're not careful to pull all the rope tight before rapping down to clean. Also, a high strength prusik will be static (for example, 5 mm cord), and unless it's super long, this will interfere with the dynamic properties of the rope; with a fall, the prusik will invert and be dragged upwards and hold the rope to the piece it's on (reducing the dynamic

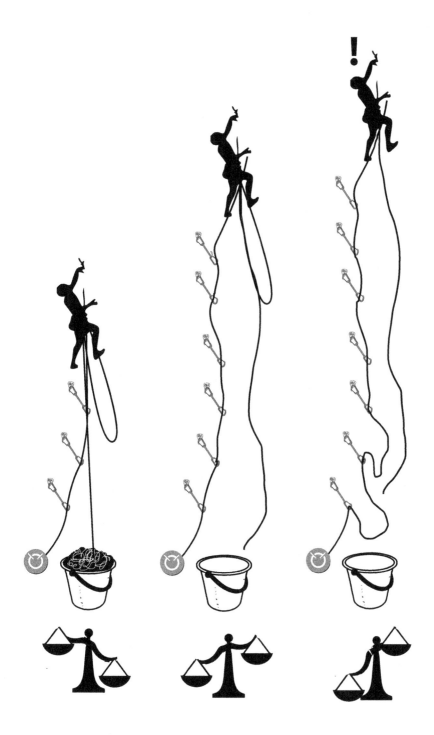

properties of the rope, as well as shocking the single piece). The ability for a force to be spread over the full length of the down rope is vital when doing hard aid.

The dynamic (stretch) properties are way more important as they will allow the rope to remain dynamic whilst doing the job. I find that the best material is either a 1.5 metre prusik loop made from 3 mm bungee cord, or a skydiver elastic band. The former is cheap, light and very stretchy, and will hold any rope well, but still stretch when loaded. The latter is a little simpler and several can be carried (you can stick them on your wrist). The bands are designed to hold your chute when packing, and although stronger than you'd imagine, they are cheap and disposable.

One item to avoid is 2 mm cord, which is neither strong or stretchy, but worse still, in my experience there is a chance it could actually cut or damage the rope! When a piece of 2 mm cord is shock-loaded with anything more than body weight, it will snap, sending one end flying away at super high speed, with enough force to slice through objects like a knife. I have used 2 mm cord loop to demonstrate bounce testing, and several times I've received deep cuts to my fingers when the cord broke (I now wear gloves).

You can, of course, simply tie a knot in the rope and clip this into a piece of protection, but again, as the rope has low stretch (unless you apply a high force), you face the same problem as using a full strength prusik. If you need to use your rope, then use an alpine butterfly and make the loop about a metre long, so as to retain some dynamic stretch in the rope. I would only really use this technique when confident I'm not going to fall (well, at least convince myself of that fact).

CROSSOVER

Error: Lead line is crossed over the haul line. If using a haul line or tag line it's vital that your haul line always remains on top of the lead line, and so it's worth getting into the habit of checking this constantly. This usually happens when you clip in the lead line to protection over the top of your haul line. Twisting them means that:You may find it hard to rap down the haul line, especially if the pitch is very steep, complex or traversing (you won't just have the rope plum to the belay). Once crossed over, when you release the haul bag it will be trapped under the lead line, so will not swing out in the direct line to the belay. If the pitch is not too complex you may be able to fix this when cleaning, but if it is, or the haul bag ends up pulling hard on your lead rope, then it could make things very tricky. Pay close attention to this if it's very windy, a heavy loaded haul line rubbing across a loaded lead line might not cut through each other, but may well prove very worrying.

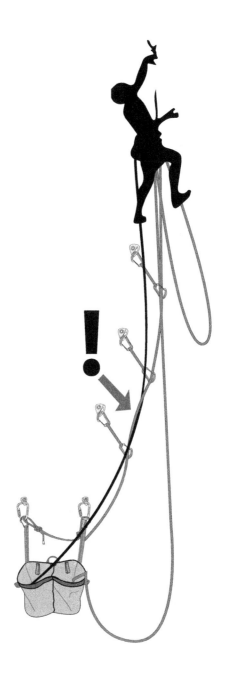

- If you are running a tagging system (a rack attached to your haul line, then crossing the ropes will bring the whole system to a halt, as you won't be able to pull the tag rack/bag around the crossedover ropes.

Avoiding the error: Whenever you clip your protection, take a moment to see where your haul line is running and that it is clear of the lead line, running free all the way to the belay below.

Sorting the problem: If you spot a crossover you will need to sort it out, usually by descending and unclipping the lead line. If you've been observant then you should be able to bend down and re-clip the lead line to free the haul line, but if not, then you'll have to rap down to sort it out. To rap mid pitch you're best to either create an intermediate belay (two pieces equalised), or tie off the rope to your highest piece, then the piece below. Clip in your belay device (and backup prusiks), unclip from your soloing device, and rap down. Once sorted, jumar back up (a good reason to lead with your jumars). As you can imagine, doing this is a nuisance and wastes a lot of time, but does help to focus the mind in the future, making you a tad more observant.

DEAD CLIPPING

Error: Dead rope is clipped instead of live rope.

Crossovers are are pain but they are not life threatening, but dead clipping is and is by far the most dangerous error a soloist can make.

Dead clipping is caused when the dead rope is confused with the live rope and the dead rope is clipped into the protection as you climb. If you fall, instead of the live rope coming tight onto the anchor, allowing the protection to arrest your fall, the dead rope is pulled through all the gear (as the rope is yanked out of its rope bag), and you take a factor 2 fall onto the belay (you fall double the height you've climbed, which could be considerable!).

Avoiding the error: To avoid this dangerous error you need to get into the habit of testing the rope each time you clip protection, giving it a tug to check it is tight to the belay. If you pull it and the rope just keeps coming up ... then you have a problem.

Sorting the problem: If you find yourself mid pitch and have the shocking realisation that you have no gear clipped (it's happened to me!), you will first shit yourself and then you will need to do something about it. The first step is to make yourself safe (if you're soloing you will probably be attached to solid gear anyway), and I would build a mini anchor and clip into it. Now pull up some of the dead rope in order to give yourself some slack in the live rope and clip this into the anchor with an alpine butterfly knot. Now you need to rap down the dead rope, clipping out the dead rope and clipping in the live rope. If you have good gear then just clip enough pieces to feel safe. Remember that, as you ascend, you will be pulling up the dead rope

through the protection you have left un-re-clipped, meaning the rope will pass through it, leaving it unattached. If you can just get this when rapping down and jugging when cleaning, that's fine, but if the gear is very marginal, it may get lost (or forgotten), so take this into account.

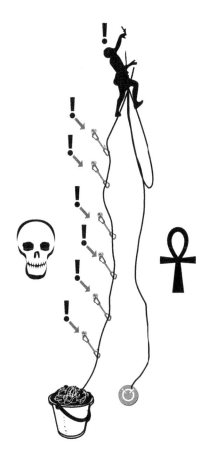

REVERSED BELAY DEVICE

Error: Device is attached incorrectly

When you're tired or in a rush it's quite easy to put on your device the wrong way, especially when using a device such as a GriGri or Soloist. Doing so means that the device will be totally ineffective if you fall, meaning you will drop onto your backup knot. Nine times out of ten you will spot your error before you move very far, as the rope will feed poorly or not at all.

Avoiding the error: Familiarity with your device (whatever it is) is crucial, but even then you can make mistakes. Try and come up with a set of rules for attaching the device, such as with a GriGri you remember that the rock is your belayer, and so the rope from the belay should be running into the 'hand' side of the device. The most important thing to do is to always check your device by giving it a yank in the ordination you will fall (do this at the belay by giving yourself some slack between the belay and the device then yank up on the rope, if the device does not lock then you've got it set up wrong).

The risk of pilot error with devices is one of the many advantages of the Silent Partner, as it's just about impossible to set it up the wrong way (it locks in all directions); a boon if you're doing speed ascents and haven't slept for 24 hours.

As a footnote, if you find you're making this kind of mistake often, then perhaps you should take a moment and reconsider your climb, fitness, speed or even the ability for you to undertake this solo ascent. If in real doubt about such things then stop.

Sorting the problem: Just clip in with knot and re-attach the device.

DEAD LINE

Error: Haul line is not clipped to belay This is another potentially fatal error and one that could see you rap off the end of your haul line! It will occur if you forget to attach the end of your haul line to the belay (the end will usually be attached to your haul bags, but not always), meaning that when you rap down after you've led the pitch, you could rap past the belay. In most situations you will not even notice this error, as the end of the haul line remains in the rope bag, but where you have a traversing pitch you will need to jumar (or at least pull yourself) back to the belay using your haul line. If the haul line is not attached as you pull on it, the rope end will just feed out of the bag and you'll swing back into space!

Avoiding the error: As with all such errors you need a good preclimb system, where you check each part of the belay before you set off (lead rope is attached, haul line is attached).

Sorting the problem: The only time this happened to me I was rapping down in a hail storm with just my shorts and t-shirt on (desperate to get to my belay and under the flysheet), but as I tried to swing back, the line just fed out of the rope bag and I was left hanging. In that situation I was lucky that I was running two haul lines, so jugging up as fast as I could, I got back to the belay and rapped down again (luckily this one was attached!). If you find yourself unable to get back to the bottom belay then you can either re-ascend to the top belay and descend via your lead line (slow), or climb back up the haul line until you can grab the lead line, and then clip into this with a daisy chain and use it as a hand-line as you rap the haul line back to the belay (you could clip in your haul line, but this may prove difficult to unclip when cleaning with your haul bag is attached).

FALL LINE

Error: On a traversing pitch the weight of your lead line between you and the tag bag leads to the rope feeding out, which can pull the fifi hook off and result in the tag bag falling (which will shock-load you).

Avoiding the error: This problem is caused when the

weight of the rope between you and the rope stacking in the rope bag (in the tag bag) becomes great enough to start feeding the rope out. I think this is often initiated by a sudden jerk as you move; as the rope feeds out it picks up some momentum, the rope feeds faster and gets heavier and, before you know it, all the rope has fed out, jerked off the fifi and your bag is falling! On a traversing pitch, keeping the tag bag close to you (keep moving it along as you climb) can help to reduce the risk of this, but often this may not be an option. Fifi hooks that can only be lifted by an upward pull (such as the Petzl Fifi) could stop the bag from being pulled off, but this design could also mean that the tag bag won't release either.

Sorting the problem: If the lead rope begins to feed out at high speed and you're running a normal set-up with a fifi hook, there is little you can do apart from pray it doesn't pull the bag off. If it does, my advice would be either to take it, or risk hurting yourself by holding the rope high and trying to take out some of the shock-load.

06 CLEANING

So you've lead your pitch, set up your belay with the haul line secured to the hauler, and backed up. Now you're ready to rap back down to clean.

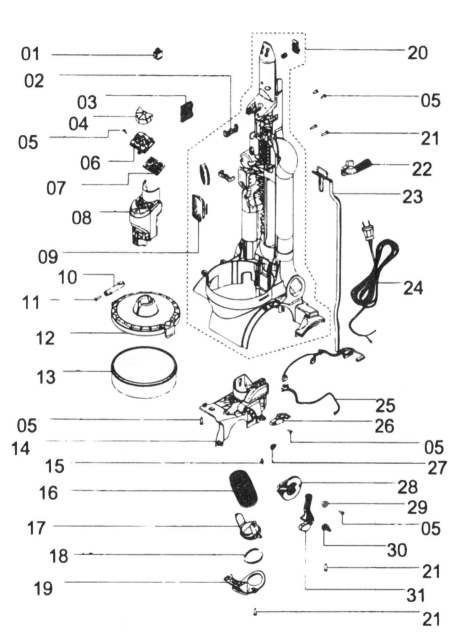

01

02

03

04

05

06

07

08

09

10

11

12

13

05

14

15

16

17

18

19

20

05

21

22

23

24

25

26

05

27

28

29

05

30

21

31

21

A few things to check before you go:

1. Make sure you leave your rack on the belay, as rapping down and jumaring up with it is a waste of energy. If you rack gear well on a sling on the way back up, you can just transfer it over once you arrive back at the top belay.

2. Make sure you have both jumars so you can jumar back up the rope. Rapping down without the jumars will happen one day, forcing you to improvise using a belay device (set in auto-lock mode) and a prusik, or better still two mini ascenders (Petzl Tiblocstyle).

3. Make sure you have your hammer, funkness device and nut tool. This is one reason why it's a good idea to attach your hammer cord to your sit harness, rather than chest harness, as it will stop you forgetting it.

Get into a routine of saying "Jumars, hammer, nut tool" before you rap down the rope.

Descending the rope

Most solo climbers (unless they are using a GriGri for lead belaying), will probably rap on a belay device, as a GriGri adds weight/bulk to your harness which could already be quite heavy. A belay device has more flexibility as friction can be increased or decreased by adding or removing krabs, meaning on a slab having one krab clipped into works best, while on an overhanging rap you may want two (to reduce your death grip on the rope).

Dead man's hand

When rapping, get into the habit of always having a backup. This is not only to stop you if you get hit by an object while rapping, but more importantly as a backup to a fuck-up! When you're tired it's very easy to make a stupid mistake, such as not clipping the rope in correctly, not doing up your screwgate properly, or any other of a million ways to die (I once put on my GriGri on the wrong way round four times on the same descent ... not good when you have a haul bag attached to you).

When rapping the haul line you can create a backup either using a prusik loop or one of your jumars, but for speed I always use my jumar, as I can clip this straight into the lead rope upon reaching the belay. With a prusik you can either clip this to your belay loop or leg loop, but on a wall I prefer the belay loop method, clipping off my belay device a few pockets higher on my daisy chain. Having a belay device a little higher than normal also allows you to see the device much better, reducing the risk of making a mistake (the real estate of a harness belay loop can be very crowded).

With a jumar this needs to be set up ready to jumar the pitch (which is what you will be doing once you reach the bottom of the rope), with an aider connected (use your lower 'foot loop' jumar). Simply rap with the ascender held above the belay device with your finger pulling the cam back from the rope (if you're really scared you can use this method and the prusik method!).

When using a prusik backup, attach this first, then pull up a little slack so as to thread your belay device without having to fight the weight of the rope. If you opt for the jumar method, you can do the same, just clip the jumar into the rope (inverted), pull in some slack and let the jumar hold it while you thread the device.

Pre-jumar set up
Before you set off down, get both jumars set up for jumaring, then if need be you can just switch modes (important if you rap too low). The bottom jumar (with aider) will probably already be clipped into the haul line as a back up, so in order to have the top jumar close at hand, clip this into your backup jumar.

Gloves
I would always keep my gloves on for hauling, cleaning and leading, so don't forget them. Also, when using a belay device on a single thick rope, things can get hot and leather gloves will help you to

control the rope better. Heat can be an even bigger problem with a GriGri, as the rope is running around a small steel cam; on a belay device, the heat is dissipated out into the chunky krabs (a good reason to double them up, as you not only increase the control friction but also heat absorption), so leather gloves are recommended (a bare hand can feel pretty puny when rapping on a GriGri over a big drop!).

To clean on the way down or not?
As you descend you will often be tempted to clean gear, but generally you should leave it until you go back up. The reasons being:

- You will simply end up having to climb back up the rope with the extra weight of gear that you could have left above you.
- You might make cleaning gear harder if you remove key pieces, especially on traverses.

- Removing gear going up on jumars is always easier, plus as you take gear out on the way down, you tend to have to swing around too much (not good for the rope). The only time I'd clean on the way down is if the gear was highly spaced and its position would make it irretrievable, but even if that was the case, you should be able to pass it on jumars, then swing back to get it.

Shake out the dead
As you descend, check the lead rope is running correctly down from the belay, especially where you have re-belayed the rope with rope stoppers. If you can do it easily, then disengage rope stoppers, so as to stop them being overly stretched when cleaning. Failure to check that the rope has no dead slack in it can result in a sudden release of slack as you jumar, which will be both very scary and could result in your jumars shock-loading the rope (not good).

Two haul lines
If you have two haul lines, then rap down on both of them, both to increase safety, but also

as a precaution that one might not be attached to the belay (again, make sure you always have your haul lines fixed to the belay, as not doing so will see you hanging in space on your rope ends!).

Regain: Getting into the belay – straight pitches

So you have rapped down your haul line until you're level with the belay. Lock off your jumar/prusik and pull yourself in until you can clip your aider/daisy chain into a bolt or the powerpoint of the belay. Once

secure, swap your backup jumar from the haul line and into the lead line. Now you are safe you can unclip your belay device and begin to strip the belay.

Regain: Getting in – overhangs and traverses

When you are unable to simply rap down to your last belay, you will need to pull yourself in somehow. If you can just pull yourself in then great, but as you get closer you will often find you're pulling yourself up with just your hands on the

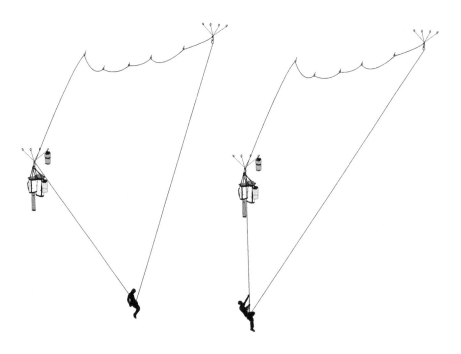

rope and ultimately slide back down.

The first thing to do is time your position correctly, as if you rap down too far below the belay, you'll end up having to jumar up (requiring both jumars); while if you go too high, you can end up stuck between a locked-off belay device/backup and your belay.

The most effective method is to clip your top jumar (clipped to your lower/foot jumar/backup) into the rope below you once you're level with the belay (which may still be tens of meters away), and begin to slowly take in the rope, pulling yourself nearer. Don't pull super tight as you might find it hard to release your backup jumar.

If it looks like you need to drop a long way below the belay in order to regain, clip a biner through the head of the jumar (making sure it's upside down so that when you lower, it will be facing the belay), then bite the bullet and clip into the rope below when level. Pull yourself as close as you can, then rap all the way until you're hanging 100% from this jumar (you'll probably be hanging in the bottom of a big V now). Swap over the jumar that was your backup (possibly now inverted) and clip it to the new 'up' rope and jumar up to the belay.

Dismantling the belay

So you're at the belay. First off, secure yourself to the lead rope, ready to jumar/clean the pitch, making sure to take in all the dead rope. Tie into the end with a figure 8 then, if using a GriGri, attach this or tie in short (you are attached at four points, but being tied to the end doesn't count as a fall to the end may kill you anyway).

Releasing the bag

The first thing to do is get the bag off the belay and onto the haul line. Invariably you will never have a tight haul line leading down to your bag, but rather a load of slack (the haul line will generally be pulled out of your rope bags when getting onto the belay). If you were to simply lower the bag out all the way, you would be wasting a great deal of energy, as every inch you lift a bag requires effort. Instead, you need to shorten the haul line so the bag loses as little height as possible. Your bag should already be set up for far-end hauling (Petzl Micro Traxion attached to the bag's suspension). First, take in all the slack with the Traxion until it's as tight as you can get it, then backup the pulley by tying a figure 8 and clipping this into the bag's suspension krab. If you don't want to use/ need a far-end hauler, you can simply pull the rope tight and tie an alpine butterfly knot and clip this into the suspension karabiner (this will never be as tight, but is safer as you don't have the Traxion in your system).

Make sure the haul-line end is detached from the belay and free (you will have several metres of haul line with which to lower out the bag; make sure the rope end is free, so it doesn't form a loop as you haul).

Now you can release the bag using the docking cord. If it's a short lower-out then just clip the lower-out/haul line into a krab, but if it's a long lower-out use a monster munter.

The bag will now swing out into space, leaving you with the belay free.

Clean the belay while hanging on your jumars and don't forget to take both rope bags (lead-rope bag for stowing rope while jugging and haul-line bag to store haul line while hauling).

Cleaning
Clean the pitch as you normally would, paying attention to rack and sort as much as possible as you go. I always rack my quickdraws on my harness ready for the next pitch and rack my gear on a sling ready to be clipped on my chest harness.

Cleaning on a GriGri: The moving 'knot'

When you clip in your jumars to clean, you can clip the top jumar on and off without tying in all the time by using a GriGri clipped to your belay loop. To begin with you will need to feed the rope through as you go, but slowly as the weight of the rope increases below the device, the rope will begin to feed itself through. This will effectively be a moving knot, increasing your safety. Using this method rather than just tying knots also allows more effective 'rope bagging' (see below), which again reduces the chances of 'hang up' with multiple rope loops below the cleaner.

Lastly, the GriGri makes a very effective cleaning tool, allowing you to lower off each piece of gear if you can't master the rope grab method. To do this you would:

1. Push both jumars close to gear, make sure GriGri is tight on the rope.

2. Take in tight on the GriGri so you're hanging from this, not the top jumar.

3. Unclip the top jumar and pass the gear (add a krab to the jumar's head hole if you think it will be loaded initially at an angle over about 15 degrees).

4. Unclip the bottom (foot) jumar and clip this in (if you can), or leave it dangling until you're able.

5. Now simply let some slack through your GriGri and you will lower out from the piece, until all the weight is on your top jumar. Then, just swing back and take out the gear.

Rope bagging

One of the biggest jobs on a wall seems to be bagging up your lead and haul lines in their rope bags. One way to reduce the time taken, as well as reduce the risk of rope ends/loops blowing onto repeating flakes, is to bag the lead line as you jug. To do this you just clip a rope bag to your harness and after tying into the end of the lead line, start feeding in the rope as you go (you will need to know where the 'bottom' of rope is as this will need to be tied to the haul line if using the continuous loop method, plus it's good practise). As you jumar, the rope will feed through your GriGri (this system works best with a GriGri), so all you need to do is carefully feed the rope down into the rope bag every 5 metres or so (packing it down with your hand will reduce the chance of the rope 'running out' again whereby the rope feeds back out of the bag when the weight of the unstuffed rope is heavier than the stowed rope). Once you reach the belay, the lead line is already fixed to the belay ready to feed out of the bag.

Using a cleaning cord

In order for you to pack your rope bag as you go you will need to avoid any big lower-out on your lead rope, especially where you will need to untie from the end and pull the rope through (the GriGri or hand method deal with the majority to short lower-outs under 2 metres). To reduce the need to use your rope you can use a cleaning cord instead, a 15–20 metre length of 6 mm cord stowed in a stuff sack (this cord can double up as a lower-out extension for your haul bag, cordelette or rap slings). The cord is thin enough to be slipped into peg eyes, bolts or other fixed gear with a krab already attached, allowing you to clean pieces without leaving junk slings behind. To set up the line, first clip in the stuff sack to a locking krab, then take one end of the cord and tie it to the krab with munter (Italian) hitch tied off securely (attachment point A). This could just be a figure 8, but having a releasable knot allows you to untie and escape from it if you misjudge the distance of a lower off more easily, or your 'pull end' jams in a lower-off. Once tied, feed in the rope until just the end is left free. This free end will be the treading end. The bag should be stowed in a small, tough, stuff sack (Fish or Metolius make some great little bags), with a clip loop so you can clip it to your harness.

To use on a lower-out, you can either use a bight of cord (a loop that will effectively reduce your total lower-out distance to ¼ your rope length), or a single strand (this gives you an effective lower-out of ½ the length).

Using the loop method, take the free end and attach it to your harness with an alpine butterfly or figure 8 (attachment point B). Now make a loop from this strand and push it through the eye of the piece you want to lower off. Clip this loop back into your harness (attachment point C) without the knot, and pulling in on the free end (feeding onto the stuff sack), pulley yourself tight until you can remove the krab and rope from the lower-out. Now you should be able to let the rope feed back through, the loops dragging as you go. If you have a 20 metre cord, then the rope will go tight after 5 metres and you will need to work something else out. Once you're lowered out simply unclip the loop (attachment point C) and the loop will pull through, freeing you from the lower-off.

To using the cord for longer lower-out, you need to feed the end through the eye of the lower-off and attach this back to your harness (with an alpine butterfly), then clip in the other side with a munter hitch and, again, pulley yourself up until you're hanging from the cord. Remove the lead rope and krab, and lower out on the cord until it goes slack (with 20 metres of cord you can lower out 10 metres), now untie both knots, pull the cord through the lower-out and store it back in the stuff sack.

Transition from cleaning to hauling and leading
Once you reach the belay you should do the following while still hanging from your jumars on the lead rope:

1. Remove the rope bag containing the lead rope and attach it to the belay, ready for leading.

2. Strip off the rack and clip it into the racking sling ready for next lead.
3. Give yourself 20 feet of lead line and clip in as a backup for hauling.

 4. Take off fail-safe on the haul line.

5. Switch jumars from the lead line to the haul line.

6. Begin hauling by the 'diver' method (or alternatives).

07 HAULING

Hauling kit from A to B is one of the most taxing elements of big wall soloing, exhausting, frustrating and sometimes potentially dangerous. If you are to succeed and thrive on a wall, then it's vital that you master all forms of hauling, as well as docking, setting up your bags and packing. In this section I will discuss all elements of moving your gear, both to and from the route, as well as up it.

Pre-wall: Preparing the pig

So all your kit has made it to the base of the wall: food, water, medical, clothing, rack – all of it in a big mess around your bag. First of all you need some order and to plan what you don't need now, what you will need now, and what you may need now! (emergency kit such as your shell, first aid supplies, water and snacks).

Task number one is to remove all the carry straps from the bag and stick them in the bottom in a stuff sack (if you're sure you won't need them before the descent). If you lose the bottom webbing straps you can use a quickdraw instead, but make sure you remember the belt!

If you have one bag, then begin by stowing water in the bottom, but if you have two bags, then spread the water around in case one is lost.

Having 2 or 3 litre bottles will create gaps and these can be filled with smaller .5 litre bottles. I like to have a cans of coke (or diabetes juice) at the end of the day, so tend to stuff these cans between my bottles, both to add more fluids, but also to protect them from being damaged. Having tough, flexible, water bladders (like those made by Ortlieb or MSR) will allow you to fill more of the available space, but these cost more than cheap bottles of water. Keep 3 litres of water near the top each day to drink. If you're on a route which is heavily travelled, then consider urinating into empty bottles so as to keep the ledges/rock clean for others (I think this should be established as 'the norm' on routes like the Nose on El Cap). Empty bottles can also be used to store trash or WAG bags (poo bags) if you run out of space in your poo tube (make a slit in the bottle then gaffer tape shut).

If you're going for an extended climb (7+ days) you'll probably need 2 bags, so fill the secondary one with kit or food you won't need until the second half of the climb, and just leave it on the bottom of your main bag.

Although some people use their sleeping mat to line a haul bag, I tend to use a sheet of Correx to line the bag, so as to make it stiff to protect the contents and stop the bag becoming damaged (it helps to reduce damage to water bottles). Cardboard can also be used but tends to only be good for one trip, plus it can get smelly if it gets damp (although you could eat it if things got desperate!). In an emergency the Correx sheeting could be used to sleep on, or be inserted into a sleeping bag for extra insulation. As for my mat, I always use a thin foam mat (won't puncture) that is cut to fit, rolled up around the inside of my bag on top of the Correx.

Setting up to haul

So your bags are packed and now you need to attach them to your haul rope ...

Swivel or not? On slabby terrain a swivel makes a difference, as it allows the bags to roll across slabs without twisting the haul line (this can lead to tangles), but hopefully, if soloing, you'll be on steeper ground, so will be off the slabs. A swivel also adds one more link in the system that could cause issues. One variation of the standard swivel is the combined swivel and locking karabiner, which work very well as they keep the locking krab/knot/suspension at the correct angle (the most dangerous angle is a krab hanging horizontal, held between both sets of straps with the haul line hung on the gate, although even then, with modern krabs this should still be safe). Attaching your haul line: There

are lots of variations when it comes to attaching a haul line, with numerous methods designed to overcome various problems, but first let's look at what we want our connection to achieve ...

1. We need a connection that offers 100% reliability, even when loaded badly.

2. We need a system that can be detached quickly so as to allow shortening/retying of the haul line, as well as allowing for the swift untangling of ropes.

3. We need a system that can be adapted to be used with pulleys, GriGris or jumars for direct hauling.

Although we could tie the bags to the haul line or attach with a taped-up maillon, the best and fastest method is to attach it with two large HMS krabs with opposed gates, as this offers redundancy as well as ease of use.

The only knot you should ever use with a haul is an alpine butterfly, as no other knot will untie easily after heavy loading – a vital requirement when shortening the haul line.

Knot protection

Your knot will need some kind of protection while on the wall and although plastic bottles work out, the best method is a heavy-duty fuel funnel. With any rope protector, remember that if you lower the bag out, you should tie the lower-out line below the knot protector, otherwise it will split apart or become damaged. Also, your knot protector should have a clip-in loop that can be attached to the knot so it isn't lost.

Docking cord

When you haul a bag up you need to be able to clip it off to a separate connector, as the hauler needs to be unclipped for the next pitch. This connector would usually be a daisy chain or sling lark'sfooted through one strap on the haul bag (this way you can still access the bag). One thing to note is that if you do use a daisy chain (personally I'd avoid it), only ever clip one pocket when clipping it in short, as the huge weight involved, as well as standing on the bag (very common), could see the bag rip a pocket, and if you've crossclipped pockets (or clipped two pockets), the bag could come free! One problem with this system when using medium to heavyweight bags is that, when the next haul is directly above, it's easy to unclip this daisy chain (the bag lifts up and the

daisy chain is unweighted and so unclipped); on traversing pitches, or when the next belay is below, your daisy chain will not be unweighted. Unclipping a weighted daisy chain in these situations requires you to either lift the whole weight of the bag by yourself or set up a mini haul (best done by clipping the lower-out line high on the belay and hauling on a GriGri or belay device).

A better alternative, and one I would recommend, is to use a docking cord. This is a 6.5 metre length of 8 mm or 9 mm dynamic rope that allows you to tie off the bags with a releasable knot, giving you both total security and a secure adjustable tie off, as well as the ability to release the bag on any belay (7 mm cord is fine on a normal or an easy wall).

To set up, double up the cord so you have two 3 metre tails, then tie an overhand knot at the bend, making the bight big enough for your hand to pass through. Before you tighten the knot, take a short length of the same cord (about 30 cm

but in a different colour), and pass this through the knot to create a second loop that is longer than the primary one (it's vital you know which is which as this will not be as strong at the primary loop). This loop will be used to clip in the bag's suspension krabs, so that when hanging from the belay, the bag is not hanging from just one strap, yet allows you to easily unclip to gain entry to the bag(s). Now lark's foot the primary loop to one strap, or if you're using two bags side by side, into one strap on both bags (see diagram).

To use, when the haul line's knot is about 20 cm from the pulley (the bags have been hauled to the belay), pull up both strands of the docking cord and tie directly into the powerpoint with a munter hitch (this reduces links in the chain, plus saves a krab; note: you need to learn to tie directly into a krab without being able to open that gate, which reduces the risk of tying a clove hitch by accident). Once done, you need to tie off the knot, which you do by taking both strand ends and wrapping them in opposite, overlapping, directions (like a maypole) around the loaded cord. After five or so wraps, tie off with a single overhand knot (not a figure 8, which could 'roll out' under load, or a quick release knot). You now have to release the load on the pulley, take off the cam and lower the weight onto the cord (untie the overhand knot completely and let the bags run out), and that's it … easy!

Whenever you have your bags attached via your docking cord, you should back this up by clipping in the haul line as well, just to have some redundancy in the system.

If you need a more shock-absorbing belay chain, then you will need to lower the bags a little (see belay section).

Carrying the hauler

If you're tagging your rack with the continuous loop method, then you can stick all your hauling kit (as well as belay stuff) in your tag bag, and so reduce the weight on your harness. If you're rope soloing with a haul line attached to the back of your harness, then you'll need to carry the hauler with you.

Far End Hauling

Before we continue I should cover adding a direct hauler to your system; this is vital for hauling on difficult/featured/slabby or problematic ground, as well as moving the bags off the wall (a good technique for vertical ground, such as on summits), and shortening the haul line before hauling. This is basically a set up whereby the leader can haul the bag from the bag end (this has various names, but let's call it 'direct hauling', as the hauler is attached directly to the bag). To do this you add a hauler directly to the haul bag, allowing you to pull the bag over roofs, obstructions etc., rather than rapping down, unsticking it, jugging back up and hauling. Using a Petzl Micro Traxion is the best method, as this allows very effective hauling in a small, solid and compact pulley. This hauler also allows rapid rope shortening before you release the haul bag (when soloing the haul bag is never hanging from the end of the haul line, rather some way along it). The far end pulley is set under the knot protector; remember to always have some slack rope after the pulley so you can haul it through (pass this through

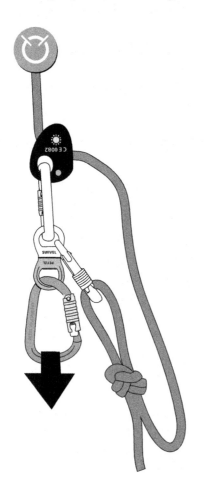

the knot protector). Never trust the pulley alone, as cams can be restricted or depressed by objects, meaning they don't lock off as they should, resulting in the bag running off the rope. To avoid this, always tie in the haul line several feet down from the pulley (see diagram) using an alpine butterfly or figure 8, tucking this spare rope into the bag so it can't hang up. If lowering out the bag from belays, leave the rope end free so it just hangs down, but make a backup knot a metre down from the pulley (see diagram).

To actually use the far end hauler if the bag gets stuck, you rap down the free lead line (or the free end of the haul line, tied-off to the belay), then with a combination of pulling on the bag, and pulling on the rope, you lift the bag high enough on the Traxion to get it past the impasse. Now you jumar back up the rope and haul. If you have multiple hang ups (say on a route like Lurking Fear on El Cap), you could just jumar on the free end of the haul line, so like a counter balance, allowing you to remain close to the bags and move them when they get stuck (remain backed up to the lead line if you do this).

Hauling light-weight bags
With a bag or tag rack below half your body weight (20–50 kg), you can try just hauling using your hands, but you'll soon get tired. An alternative is pulling the load up as you would a lazy climbing partner. Putting the rope through a krab will make it a little easier, but a GriGri, Tibloc or guide plate in auto-lock mode will give you the ability to take rests as you pull up the load. An alpine clutch (see diagram) is an alternative method, but personally I find I never have the right krabs to make it work as they need to be the same shape. The best method is just to employ a mini pulley (or a large one of that's what you have) such as the Petzl Micro Traxion, as hauling is what it does well and it will save you time and effort. With a light load you can usually just pull the rope through the pulley using

gloved hands, with one pulling the up strand to the other the down strand. Unfortunately, aside from speed ascents and rack hauling, most of your hauling will be of the medium- to heavy-weight variety!

Hauling medium-weight bags
Before we get into this, remember that even if you were planning on taking twice as long on a wall as with a partner, you will only be hauling a bag as heavy as on a partnered ascent, as you carry half the water used by a two man team. This means that if you've managed on team ascents of walls (let's hope you have!) then you can handle most solo walls.

This book is not designed as a standalone 'how to climb a big wall', but for completeness I'll cover what I feel works for hauling. The three most effective ways to haul are what I call the 'diver' haul (my favourite) and the 'squat' haul (not as easy, but works when a diver haul is not possible) and the hip haul (good for lighter loads).

Diver haul: This is called a diver haul as it reminds me of free-divers pulling themselves down lines in order to get further into the deep, and is basically a 'space haul' without a second person hauling. To do this, you simply attach yourself to the haul line with both jumars, using a length of lead line as a backup (the length depends on how far you want to drop). Once secure, you use your body weight as a counter balance (so your bags need to be close to your own weight, give or take), and grabbing the up rope (the loaded rope coming up from the bag), you begin hauling yourself downwards. With this system you can raise a bag very quickly with minimal energy as long as you can jumar well. Pull down until your backup goes tight, jug up, then repeat.

Squat haul: A squat haul is harder work and uses your body weight less effectively, making more use of the arms and legs. With this system you are effectively using a rope grab (a GriGri is best, or a jumar) clipped to your harness to pull the rope through the pulley. Either by squatting or half squatting down (you can press against the wall with your arms, or even press out using your feet), you pull in 30 cm to 60 cm of haul line through the pulley. You then pull yourself back up, pulling the rope back through your GriGri and repeat (having a jumar clipped to the powerpoint so you can pull up on its handle is great). The best thing about using a GriGri is that, once the bag needs to be lowered onto the docking cord and the pulley's cam is released, you can easily let out the slack (it takes a bit more practise with a jumar).

Hip haul: This haul is set up as with the squat, but tends to work best with a GriGri clipped directly to the harness leg and waist so as to give maximum distance between hauler and GriGri, this is designed to maximise the amount of pull your hips have from you to the pulley. To haul, use a combination of pressing away with your hands (like a standing press up) and pulling with your hips (the overall effect is a cross between having sex and having a crap), pulling the rope through about 30 cm at a time. With each pull you will need to take in the slack with the GriGri. This is best done by clipping the end of the rope coming out of the GriGri through a krab high on the belay, so you're able to pull down on the rope and pulley as you move back to your start position. Although you're only pulling in a small amount of rope at a time, this technique requires very little movement or energy (compared to the squat haul), and works well with lighter load; it is especially good in hot weather when hauling can sap what strength you have left.

Hauling heavy-weight bags

If you're very light, or climbing the biggest of walls (10+ days), then you may find that none of the medium-weight options work for you, or not at the start at least (remember that your bags will get lighter each day as long as you drink water). In these situations you have multiple choices in order to manage the heaviest of loads. I learned that, on most walls, you need to employ different haul techniques depending on what the situation dictates.

Double haul: This is one of the simplest heavy-weight hauling methods and personally one I find the most effective, as the weight of each bag tends to be less than in a medium haul and using the diver haul method means they come up fast. In order to do a double haul without the weight of having two haul lines attached to your harness, you need to use it as part of the continuous loop system (so the haul lines aren't attached to you directly).

Both haul lines need their own rope bags feeding up from the belay when leading, and I would split bags into your main bag then a second bag that holds the second half of your food and water (so you don't have to open it).

The only technical detail that needs covering (as you can haul the bags any way you want), is preparing the haul line attachment at the top belay before rapping. If you have two pulleys you could set up both bags with one each, but normally you only have one. Hang one bag from a pulley as normal, but from a second HMS krab, tie the haul line in with a munter hitch, then tie this off with at least a metre of slack; back this up by tying a figure 8 into the slack and clip off again (so that if your munter tie-off failed, the bag would not run out and fall). Once you have hauled the bag (A) onto the hauler and secured it,

1. Remove it's haul line (bag A) from the hauler (without taking the hauler off the powerpoint).

2. Untie the figure 8 backup from bag B and attach this to the hauler (make sure it runs in the correct direction).

3. Attach a jumar to a long quickdraw and clip this to the powerpoint.

4. Clip the jumar (inverted) into the haul line in order to act as a rope grab (holding the bag).

5. Now untie the knot tying off the munter hitch and lower the weight of the bag onto the jumar.

6. Remove the munter hitch from the HMS and remove the HMS from the powerpoint.

7. Take in the slack on the hauler until the weight is off the jumar.

8. Remove the jumar and quickdraw and start hauling.

One bad point with the system is that you add 35% more rope handling/stuffing to your system, but on a big route this is offset by the fact you add an extra rope to your system for fixing/replacement lead rope. 3:1 pulley: Using three pulleys in your system can make a heavy single haul feel a lot easier, reducing the weight by a factor of three (so a 150 kg haul bag only needs a 50 kg pull). The downside is that the rope hauled through your top

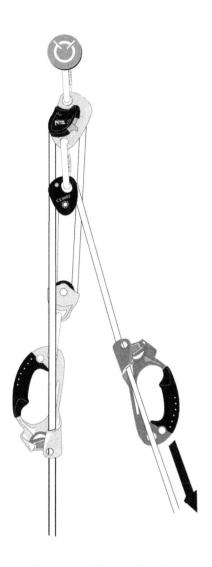

is not an option really when you're soloing). Saying that, I have used this system to do single hauls for a five person team with seven days' water (a load close to the safe working limit of the pulley).

To set up, use two medium-sized (not tiny crevasse-rescue-kit-sized) pulleys sheave mounted on sealed ball bearings (such as the Petzl Rescue, Partner or Mini); Use in combination with a Petzl Pro Traxion (the first pulley in the system, as well as your rope holder). You can use a Micro Traxion in the system as well, as this gives you a spare locking pulley. The whole system can be put together just using gear at hand, but the more in line things are, the more efficient it will be (clipping a pulley into the bottom of the Pro Traxion works well). The bottom pulley should be attached to either one of your jumars, or carry a Petzl Croll or Basic to do the job. Clipping a little weight to the Croll/Basic (such as a large cam), will weigh it down so that it runs back down the rope each time you let off the main pulling jumar.

pulley only lifts the bag by a ratio of 1:3 (so 60 cm of rope would mean you only lift the bag 20 cm). The 3:1 system can be pretty slow and frustrating and on a team ascent I always opt for space hauling (but this

How you pull the haul line through the pulley depends on you and the load, but variations of the squat and hip haul, plus the diver method, can work if you create a long enough 'Z' in your pulley

Chongo 2:1 system: This is quite a complex way of hauling that requires quite a bit of gear, a perfect set up and a lot of practise to make it work well; if you manage this, you will have a system that can take some of the grind out of hauling, which is ideal for small/light climbers or climbers with big loads. The Chongo 2:1 (or Chongo wall ratchet) was developed over many years, on many walls, by various people (including rescue teams). Over time the concept has been tweaked in order to squeeze every last drop of performance from the system, as any kink in performance is multiplied in reverse (a 10% increase in resistance due to a poor pulley would be 20% in use due to it being a 2:1 system). Chongo (a homeless big-wall philosopher and slackliner), is most often

given the credit, as he spent a lot of time coaching big-wall newbies on the technique, hanging around Camp 4 (most often on the pretext of selling on a copy of his 'Ground Manual' photocopied big-wall book).

This concept is a simple one, to create a separate compact, light and effective hauling system remote from the haul line. In doing this, a thinner (5 mm dyneema or 5mm Mammut Pro cord), more static, lower friction rope can be employed, with a 2:1 system giving greater speed than a 3:1 on the haul line, but with almost the same (or greater) efficiency due to the total focus on each component of the system.

System components: To set up you need to invest in some good gear, as throwing in cheap pulleys or the wrong krabs will lower the overall efficiency of the system. To make a Chongo 2:1 you need the following items:

• 1 x Petzl Micro Traxion (Pro

Traxion or Mini Traxion also work, but a smaller pulley allows greater travel for the system).

• 2 x Petzl Rescue Pulleys (only use medium-sized high quality pulleys mounted on sealed bearings, not small emergency pulleys).

• 5 x metres of 5 mm dyneema cord or 5 mm / 6 mm Mammut Pro cord (this is your 'Z' cord).

• 1 x rap ring (used to stop the whole system falling apart).

• 1 x metre of 7 mm cord

• 1 x Petzl Basic or Croll (a Croll can do double duty for jugging freehanging fixed lines

. • 1 x 10 mm alloy maillon (wrap some finger tape around the locking barrel to make it easier to unscrew).

• 1 x micro locker (main connector to the powerpoint).

• 1 x large HMS (Petzl William). How to use: With the system setup, you (as in the diagram)

clip the haul line into the Petzl Micro Traxion (this is the 'catch' that will be used to 'hold' the load each time you reset the pulley), then clip the Croll/ Basic into the haul line (this is the 'grab' that will pull up the load, with the Traxion 'holding'

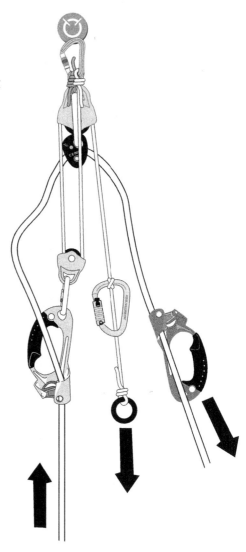

it when its reset). Now attach yourself to the 'Z' cord with a clove hitch directly to your belay loop (you will need to fine-tune this as you go). Press the Croll down on the haul line (take all the slack out of the system, as one inch will be magnified twice), and pull the 'Z' cord. The bags should rise easily (or more easily) with only half the force needed compared to a 1:1 system. Once the Croll has lifted the bag, pull the rope tight through the Traxion and pull down the cross to reset it.

Hauling point positioning
With no one to help you it's vital that you always set up the most efficient pull possible when hauling, which means the rope goes as directly as possible from the pulley wheel to the load. Any kind of edge, feature or added friction will greatly increase your workload, further sapping your strength. When setting up a haul, always work out the position that will reduce these factors, especially on walls where you have multiple belay positions (Camp 5 on the Nose for example). A prime example of how you can reduce your workload is when hauling on ledges. Usually it's a great relief when you reach a ledge, and being able to stand and haul is always nice. The problem with this scenario is that the edge of the ledge will greatly add to the difficulty of hauling, in other words, the more acute the angle, the greater the resistance. To avoid this consider extending the haul point over the edge of the ledge.

OTHER SYSTEMS

Speed hauling

I will include this technique for the sake of completeness, although personally I think it's too risky. The basic concept is that you hang your haul bag, or a lighter secondary bag, from a fifi hook attached to a second haul line. When you get to the top you clip this rope through your hauler and, rapping down your other haul line, you use your body weight to lift the bag and raise it to the belay as you go, the idea here is that you make use of your body weight. It doesn't take too much imagination to figure that this is a highly dangerous technique. The bag can (and has) fallen off the belay, due to either being knocked off (by a rock fall or a jammed rope), or by gear failure (the fifi snapped!).

If you want to play around with this technique, then here are a few pointers:

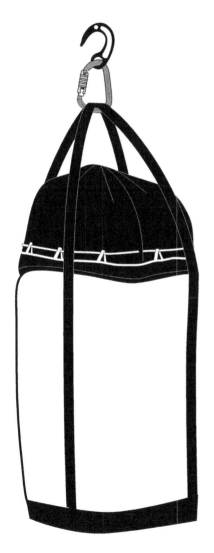

• Use two fifi hooks taped together for strength (thread the lifting cord through both hooks) or use a krab with a pronounced hook design and remove the gate and attach a webbing loop to lift it.

• Learn to tie a slippery hitch knot, as this will reduce the chance of the bags going the distance if they do pop.

• Only employ the system with the continuous loop method, as this means you won't have two haul lines clipped to you.

I don't like this system as there is much can go wrong; no one would dare haul their main bag like this, so why not just haul everything together and avoid the risk?

Alpine-style hauling

With this method you carry your load on your back; its only really of use for speed climbing, situations when you're going for the top on capsule-style routes or when you have to ferry kit over ground that is impossible to haul over. The main thing to mention is that carrying a load on your back is tough, and dangerous if the weight means you lose your style and rhythm, causing wear on the rope. I will keep this short, as most soloists will never need to carry anything on their back.

What kind of load? Anything that weighs anything will feel heavier and heavier as you climb, so keep it light. I would ideally only jug with a bag that weighs 5 kg or so, unless I was on very slabby ground; once you get on free-hanging ropes, you really need to have nothing on your back.

Ideal terrain: The best terrain for carrying loads is slabby ground or anything just off vertical. You need to have the weight on your legs for it to be most effective, as once it tips to vertical, there is always too much strain on your upper body, which is knackering.

Set up: If you know you will have a section where you must jumar with a bag on your back, then try and keep your haul bags medium sized, as having a huge wheelie-bin-of-a-bag on your back is not good. Try and keep the load down, even if this means shuttling backwards and forwards, and try and have the bag close to your back, with the weight low.

As the ground gets steeper you will feel the bag pulling you back. One way to reduce this, as well as giving you a rest, is to clip some long quickdraws through the shoulder straps and into your top jumar's daisy chain. This helps to keep the load close to the rope, as well as taking the weight of the load itself if you sag down onto it.

Russian style

Developed by the Russians for carrying loads on gnarly technical faces, this is a variation of the alpine style and is used when you don't want to or simply can't haul. With this system you basically attach the load to your belay loop and hang it down so that it's below your feet (otherwise your feet will tangle with it). This setup can be used with the Texas-style jumar system (two handled jumars), but works better with the Frog setup (one handled jumar and a Croll); as with any system it requires practise and strong legs!

Lazy haul

I've used this system quite a few times when I've been forced to climb a fixed rope while carrying something (a small haul bag for example), rather than hauling, and it works well on free-hanging ropes. To do this you attach your jumars as you would normally and tie into the end of the rope. In the loop of rope you have between your jumars and the knot at your harness you attach your load via a locking pulley (such as Petzl Micro Traxion). As you climb the rope, the loop will travel up with you, and as it does, the load will come tight on it. All you need do is keep pulling up the load as you go (in effect you have a 1:1 pulley system beneath you). This system can work very well when topping out on steep slabby ground, even with heavy loads.

Walking the dog haul

If you have to climb a fixed rope and can't haul or don't want to use any of the above systems (the lazy haul won't work on a fixed rope as you can't tie into the end), then you can use the dog-walking method. Attach the load to the rope with a locking pulley and attach a long sling or untied cordelette to it, creating a leash. Each time you climb and the leash goes tight, pull up the load and let it hang on the fixed rope. Climb on and repeat. This method can be very effective, but it's best to keep the load light

08 BIVYS

Solo bivys on a wall are pretty much the same as with partners - a chance to recharge your batteries at one of the best camping spots on the planet. Never the less, there are a few things worth thinking about

Stuff sacks

Being organised is always vital on any wall, but when you're alone doubly so. Having loads of heavy-weight stuff sacks (not light-weight sleeping bag ones) with full-strength clip loops is vital on a wall if you're not going to lose stuff. Make sure they are different colours and different types (Fish, Metolius, Alpkit etc.). Keep food in one, personal kit in another and your sleeping bag and sleep stuff in a third. Try and avoid having loose items in your bag and use a grab bag in the top (this can be attached to the lid of the haul bag) with things such as food, sunblock, water (a few .5 litre bottles take up less space than a huge 3 litre one), head torch etc. Having everything in bags (apart from water) makes it much safer to unpack on hanging belays, ledges and portaledges. Keep all clothes and sleeping kit in a secondary waterproof stuff sack within the heavy duty one and never trust crappy plastic loops sewn onto flimsy webbing on stuff sacks ... they do break!

Tethers

If you're going to hang anything from your haul bag, such as a portaledge bag, secondary bags, poo tube etc., then employing a cord tether makes things much safer. These strands of cord (7mm works well) are attached to the bags, either tied direct or clipped to their suspension krabs, and eliminate the risk of dropping the item when pulling up from below (have different colours for easy identification). Simply unclip the item when hanging under the bag, then pull it up once you get back up to the belay.

Portaledge

Make sure you can put your ledge and fly up by yourself, and not just in the garden, but hanging in your harness. Some popular ledges are very hard to assemble (even with a partner) especially if you're using a double ledge by yourself. Fly sheets that are said to be cut to fit the ledge often feel too small, and you may be forced to apply a huge amount of force to get it to fit. The best ledges for solo climbing are those made by Fish; they also tend to be the lightest, cheapest and most compact.

Packing the ledge

Pack your portaledge with a daisy chain lark's-footed into the main suspension point, so you can easily adjust the height when hanging up at night. Clip in a locking krab and leave it attached also, so you're not scrabbling around for one in the dark. You can also clip this daisy chain to you, as this will reduce the chance of you dropping it, plus having the ledge hanging from the end of the daisy chain makes it easier and safer to put up. Avoid putting your fly on the outside of your haul bag as it will get damaged, and if it has a tent pole, then tape a clip loop to it and stow it somewhere safe, ideally in a pocket inside the ledge's hauling bag (if it's loose inside, you have a good chance of losing it when you pull out the ledge).

Custom ledge bag

No one makes the ideal haul bag for a ledge and fly, but you can easily make one up yourself using heavy-weight cordura from an outdoor fabric supplier (such as Point North in the UK).

This is a two-ended tube-style bag, about 20% bigger than an off-the-shelf model, and designed to store both the

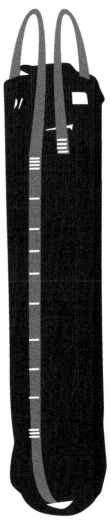

ledge and the fly in one bag. The design is much easier to use by a solo climber and provides significantly more safety due to faster reaction time in a storm. The bag holds the ledge already attached to the flysheet (use an alloy maillon taped closed), with the ledge extracted from the bottom of the bag, not the top (the bag always stays clipped to the suspension). Just pull out the ledge and leave the fly inside the bag (use the bag's bottom cord to secure the bag in place).

To stow the bag away, take the ledge apart, pull up all the parts together, then slip the bag back down over the whole assembly. Having a loop (30 cm) of medium-weight bungee with a light accessory krab attached to one corner of your ledge can be handy, as once pulled together, you can wrap this around everything and clip the loop back into itself, keeping the ledge together as you pull down the bag and secure it.

09 DESCENT AND RETREAT

Getting down from the top of any wall can prove to be one of the hardest parts of a solo ascent; this is where fitness, planning and patience can pay dividends. It is also one of the more dangerous paths a solo climber must traverse, so always factor the descent into your planning, giving yourself the time and resources to carry it out.

A FILM BY NICOLAS ROEG

THE MAN WHO FELL TO EARTH

This section covers standard non-too-overt technical descents, and any involving more complex ground (such as descending the route), will be covered in retreat.

DESCENT

Don't rush it: When you are near the top of your route, all you will be able to think about is getting down, dreaming of soft beds, hot food and showers (enough to overcome any cruxes you may encounter). The problem is that you always seem to end up topping out at around mid afternoon, or later than you think you will, and the descent becomes a crazy rush. Remember that you will be more tired than you feel and that the descent, when tackled alone, will take much longer than you think. Add a huge load (usually split with a partner), and you will end up bushwhacking in the dark, wishing you were back on the wall.

My advice would always be to bivy at the top of the wall and give yourself a full day to make the descent. This way, you will have the maximum daylight, enough time to pack your bags well for walking, and be a little more rested. If it's a blind descent and you have time, think about shuttling a load down a short way while doing a recon of the trail.

At the top of some walls you may find wood, so it's always worth carrying a lighter and a knife so you can make a small fire (a light sili tarp is also nice to have). The one time you may need to rush down is if you're out of food or you feel you are in danger (perhaps you're soaked to the skin), in this case it's best to just take your survival kit (sleeping bag, bivy bag, stove, food, mat, head torch, money, car keys etc.), and get down as fast you can, coming back later for your kit. I once saw a crazy guy top out on the Nose after a very stormy solo ascent, his only storm gear was a down jacket, his footwear a pair of Teva sandals. He was so past it on the last pitch that, as soon as he reached the tree at the top, he just untied from the rope and walked away, leaving all his rack, haul bag and ropes behind!

How to get down? When planning a solo climb make sure you have the descent wired, as at the end you will have the least energy to deal with any unforeseen problems. Consider a recon of the descent beforehand, either walking up to the summit, or climbing another route with a partner (or an easier route alone). The route down from El Cap is a great example of a route that can seem simple when you've done it, but impossibly complex when doing it in the dark for the first time, every cairn a false trail.

If you undertake a recon, make sure you scope out a good bivy spot as close to the top as possible and consider leaving a cache of food and water if you think you might need it. If there are no cairns and you're in a remote location, then consider making cairns on the way back down from the summit (you can topple them on your way down the final time); marking your route on a map is also a good idea.

If your route ends at a trailhead, but starts on the other side of the mountain, then you might need to be creative with your transport, perhaps stashing a bike there, so you can ride back to your car to pick up your gear. Taxis can be handy, but you will need a line of communication.

Splitting your load: Ropes, hardware, a portaledge and fly … you can be left with quite a load at the top of a wall, too much for one person to carry. Overload yourself with a giant haul bag and walk down slabs and screes, and you're asking for trouble. A better option is to split the load and either make two carries on alternative days, or shuttle the bags down one after the other.

If you're going to split the load, make sure you bring all the items you may need down, including survival gear, in a wilderness area. Make sure you leave your other bag where it will be easy to find and be aware of it getting buried (use your portaledge fly pole or clip stick as a wand), blown away (tie it to something and cover it with rocks), or chewed by animals (stick it in a tree).

Don't make the load equal in weight if you're feeling tired, but instead carry a lighter load down; you can return for the heavier load once you've had a chance to recover. When splitting loads I always make sure each one has a rope with it, as this can be used for rapping unforeseen drops or lowering the bags if problems occur.

If shuttling loads, make them equal weight, and try and keep the legs short (10 minutes down with one bag, leave it near a feature, walk back up and bring back the second one, passing the first for 10 minutes and repeat).

On some descents I've done a mix of both styles of retreat, shuttling the bags half way down, then leaving one bag so as to get down in the light. I shall attest to just how grateful you are the following day, when you only have to walk half way up!

Back the way you came: If the descent from a climb is very complex or dangerous (perhaps it involves creviced terrain), or is very long, then it may be worth considering descending back down the route itself, especially if you have really heavy bags. To do this you are best off employing a capsule-style of ascent, allowing you to fix up from a high camp, tag the top, then retreat back down the wall at your own pace. This, however, should not be seen as a soft option, as descending a wall alone is full of dangers and difficulties, such that can only be tamed by care and patience.

Helping hands: Although the ideal is for you to climb and descend the wall alone, sometimes having a little help on the descent makes a big difference, especially if you've got a huge load. Faced with two carries out, simply someone meeting you at the top to help you is one of the greatest things a friend can do. In some places, such as Yosemite, you can pay a 'porter' to meet you at the top, but it will cost you.

RETREAT
Retreating from a wall solo must be one of the most complex and

difficult operations any climber can undertake. On a steep or overhanging wall, getting down with a partner (never mind alone) can feel almost impossible, requiring down-aiding, bag lowering and total control of all your kit. Alone on the wall these difficulties are compounded massively and it's worth asking yourself if you feel you could retreat from a wall with a partner before even considering retreating alone.

Do I stay or do I go?

Low down on a wall, when you know the ground is still close, it's easy to begin to think about how much you miss the good life back on the deck, and so it's easy to bail (especially if you have an excuse like bad weather, flat batteries in your iPod, or you just decide you've gone off the idea). If you really feel your heart is not in it, and even if you have a genuine reason for bailing, I would always leave my ropes fixed. This may be a pain, as you will have to come all the way back up to get them, but you will be fresher and in better control of your senses.

The bottom line is never retreat in haste. The best option, unless it's a 'keeper', is to tie all your ropes together and try to fix them down to the ground so at least you are committed totally to giving up. A 60 metre lead, haul and zip line will get you a long way down off any wall ... believe me. You can rap with a bag if you want (holding all your personal stuff), leaving your food and water on the wall. Once down, at least you have the option to decide that you want in, or return to retrieve the rest of your kit when things are less frantic. Of course this also means you need to be able to pass knots, and get back up the ropes, so don't leave your jumars on the belay!

Higher on the wall you must understand just how hard and exposed a retreat will be (perhaps it takes a descent to understand how hard a descent will be). Getting you and your kit down a wall takes a huge amount of skill and hard work, often requiring you rap and jumar multiple pitches, along with down-aiding. Usually it's best to take a rest day to consider your options before committing (a day off will often see things feeling a lot better).

Abseil device? A GriGri is OK with light loads, but only works on single ropes and can be hard to use with heavy loads. A belay device with the rope running over two lockers gives good control and heat dissipation as the weight gets higher.

Solo retreat

Getting off a wall alone is going to take patience, energy and a wellthought out strategy. The following technique was used by me when descending alone from the Troll Wall, along with a ton of baggage.

First rationalise all your gear, disposing of everything that is not necessary. On the Troll Wall I used a small parachute to throw off all my non-life-support gear, but this can be risky if you end up not getting down (at least one soloist has died of hypothermia on El Cap while trying to retreat).
If the wall is vertical or better still slabby, then you can clip your haul bag to your daisy chain (clip your belay device in the middle so you are hanging off one end of the daisy chain with the bag on the other). Using a prusik as a backup, you should be able to descend down the wall; be warned ... trying to swing or pendulum with a haul bag attached to you is tough!

Down fixing: If the wall has traverses or is overhanging, then you're probably going to have to down fix. To do this you feed your ropes as normal for rapping, but tie them off in order to allow you to jumar back up once the rope is fixed. Now you go down the rope carrying your rack (don't forget your jumars!), swinging in if need be and clipping the rope above you into gear in order to get you to the belay. The trick on such descents is to never allow yourself to get so far away from the wall that you are unable to get back. To keep in contact, keep kicking in and out, and be very pro-active about clipping the rope in. If you find you go too far and lose contact, then you will need to jug back up a way and start again. If you rap with a GriGri then you can just attach a jumar and foot-loop and jumar back up.

Once you reach the belay you should fix both rope ends (you can leave the rack here) and jumar back up the ropes, taking the gear out as you go, so that the rope just runs free from belay to belay. Now you untie the knots and rap with the bag(s), attach them to the belay and pull the ropes.

Super heavy bags: If you have multiple bags and they are really heavy then you may want to have a docking cord on them, tying them on with a tied-off munter hitch when you reach the next belay. When you leave, set up to rap, then untie the munter and lower bags until they are hanging from your daisy chain/belay device, and go.

Monster munter lower: If you have multiple ropes and want to get down to the ground as fast as you can, you can just lower your bags down and then come back later to clean the ropes without having to deal with the bags. To do this you need a very

large HMS krab and enough ropes to get down (of course!). Tie all your ropes together with an overhand knot (leave 6 inches of tail), and lower the bags using a monster munter hitch (a munter hitch tied twice). As the knot gets close, you can feed it through the munter, allowing you to pass it easily (some forcing is needed with fingers, just make sure they get trapped!).

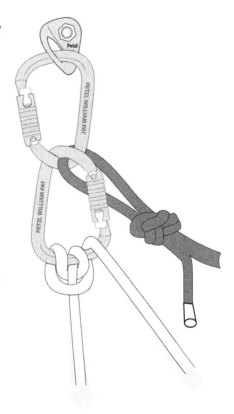

Once the bag is down you can just rap the rope.

Retrievable monster munter lower: This is a variation of the fifi death hook retrievable abseil, only this time it's used to lower your bags and then get the rope end back (hopefully). To do this you need a fifi hook and some bungee cord (you can extract some from a jacket in an emergency). Attach the bungee cord through the top hole in the fifi, then tie the fifi into the end of the rope with an overhand knot. Now tie the other end of the bungee to the rope with a prusik knot, this will be the end you lower. Set up the monster munter and hook your haul bag onto the inverted fifi hook, then pull the bungee loop tight via the bungee. You can now lower the bag as before, passing the knots. When the bag reaches the floor the weight will come off the fifi and the bungee will flick it off, allowing you to retrieve the rope end and rap. If the bag does not release then you just rap the line as before.

Throwing the bags: It's illegal to throw bags in Yosemite, plus it's downright dangerous on any busy wall (but at the cost of destroying or losing all your kit, it's a great way to speed things up on an alpine or wilderness wall!).

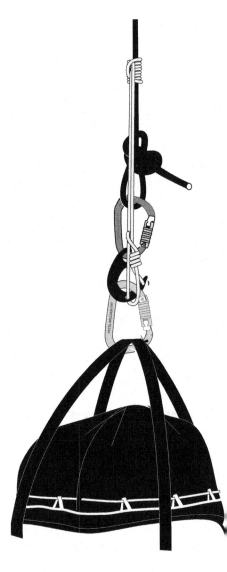

You can either toss the bags without any form of deceleration or use a parachute. With either option, you should do the following in order to have a chance of saving your bag. • Leave the lid of the bag undone so the air is forced out. Shut it and the bag will explode!

• Tie everything inside together so that if the bag blows on the way down, everything will stay together as is falls down the wall.
• Place plastic bottles with their lids just slightly twisted on in the bottom of the bag.
• Next, place the soft objects such a flysheets and spare clothes, as they will absorb the force.
• Lastly, place the heavier objects, but be aware that anything heavy may damage what lies underneath when it hits the ground.
• Don't throw anything that could be damaged, such as a portaledge, cams or anything you'd prefer not to get lost or broken into a thousand pieces (a Russian team threw off a haul bag that held all their film from Trango and it was never found).

If you go for a parachute, buy something that isn't too big, as you don't want it floating away; it's there to slow the bag down, meaning you want more of a drogue chute. You can buy these as military surplus or make your own (a good source of info, or for drogues themselves, is hobby rocket websites or companies such as www.therocketman.com).

03

{ Beyond The Wall }

01 ALPINE WALLS

Moving your soloing from safe, sunny, walls to more alpine environments adds a great deal of complexity, difficulty and danger to the alpine game, and soloing such walls as hard routes on the Jorasses, Eiger and Matterhorn requires the greatest level of skill (plus elephant-sized balls!).

CHANGING THE GAME

On an alpine wall you tend not to have the steep overhanging ground you might encounter on non-alpine walls, requiring a higher level of skill at free climbing while self-belaying; this also makes hauling more complex. You will have to carry far more equipment, including winter clothing and mixed climbing gear. Luckily, the weight carried is often lower than on a wall, as little or no water is needed because snow can be melted. Weight is still an issue however, as you may be forced to carry or ferry bags over low-angled terrain, and so having your kit split over a few medium bags works best (two 60 litre haul bags for example). The time spent on alpine walls will invariably need to be shorter than when on a normal big wall and speed is vital in order to climb in between bad weather; I would advise learning to speed solo before embarking on any big alpine solos. The exception to this would be the soloing of winter alpine walls, where you might need to spend a week or more grinding your way up the climb.

Dangers

Alpine walls add a great many environmental factors that can make things much dicier, with unpredictable ice and rock falls, as well as lightning to deal with. Loose rock is more dangerous when soloing as you will usually be climbing on a single rope, plus belays can prove much more time consuming to create. On the plus side, with a very long rope you can often link many pitches on one, and if you're slick, it could be argued that you're safer.

Exposure on an alpine wall should always be taken into account and having extra clothing as well as a belay jacket and spare mitts/gloves is a good idea. Always have a head torch somewhere close and have a strategy worked out for all eventualities: What if your lead rope gets chopped by a rock? What if you fall and break your ankle? What if you get 10 metres from the top and have to retreat?

The main thing to never forget is, although there is no shame in backing off, there is in dying!

If you can push through all the difficulties and apply your skills well, then soloing an alpine wall, or even simply attempting to solo one, can be immensely rewarding.

Capsule style

Soloing a wall beyond the safety of Yosemite Valley, where a rescue can arrive in an hour or so, you need to up your game when it comes to safety. On a remote wilderness or alpine wall, being caught out in a storm, overtaken by night, or injured, you need a better system than the 'sport' system employed on El Cap. One of the best ways to increase your margin is to go capsule style, a method of tackling huge objectives, employed by big wall teams on the hardest routes.

With 'capsule style', you are fixing ropes from a camp and when these ropes run out, or you hit a good camp, you move everything up and repeat until you hit the top. This system is slow and secure and allows the soloist to quickly rap down the fixed rope back to camp, so no having to haul, set up camp etc.

If a storm hits or you get injured, you can be back on your ledge in no time.

Capsule-style skills can be used on normal walls as well, like when you reach a good ledge and want to fix up for a day or two, and return to the ledge at night. It's also good if you're facing a storm and want to play it safe, fixing up and leaving a camp fixed until you know you'll make it off the wall (getting caught in a storm when your life support is a pitch below, all in haul bags, can be dangerous).

Capsule basics: The gear you take on a capsule ascent is the same as any other with the exception of ropes. On capsule-style routes I've climbed in the past, I've taken two 60 metre lead ropes (10.5 mm) and two 9 mm static ropes for fixing and hauling. Two lead ropes are taken because your ropes can more exposed to rock fall and wear on an alpine wall and so having a spare is a good idea.

Thicker static ropes would be nicer, but if you're carrying them to the wall by yourself, the difference between a 9 mm and 10 mm static is considerable. A

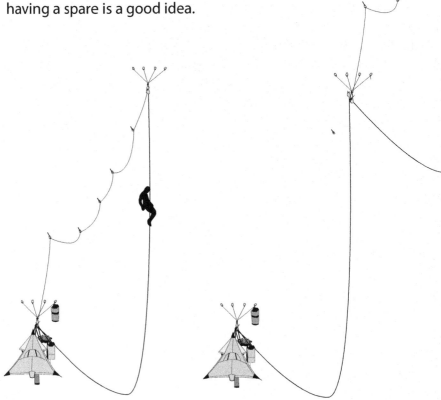

9mm static rope might sound skinny, but by the time you're ready to solo a big alpine wall, you'll be able to look after such ropes.

As you climb you fix these ropes up the wall (a 60 metre rope will usually span two or even three pitches), allowing you to push your rope four or five pitches above you before you're forced to move camps. Add your two lead ropes and that's a long way up the wall!

When fixing these ropes, employ 're-belaying' techniques when you can, attaching the static line to gear with alpine butterfly knots so as to reduce wear (ideally a fixed rope should not be loaded hard over any edges). You might also want to use edge protectors, though in my experience these are just a pain to use (the roller design that wraps around the rope is best if you do), and should be reserved for the sharpest edges.

Moving camp: Moving camp when you're soloing capsule style can either be a doddle or a total pain in the arse and there are two systems you can use once your camp is packed away (ideally in one large haul bag). You can either haul them conventionally, which will require attaching your spare rope to the bags, jumaring up and setting it up to haul from the top of the first static, then rapping downand releasing it (a lot of work), or you can use

a much easier but potentially dicey method:

Long haul method: With this method you attach the end of the fixed line to the bags, then have the bags hanging from a fifi hook attached to the static (use a slippery hitch as a backup). Begin jumaring the static ropes, taking out the re-belays until you are at the very top of your ropes (the very top of all fixed ropes). Now you can begin to haul and once the fifi lifts off the anchor, the bags will swing out and you will be able to bring them all the way to the belay in one long haul (passing the knot).

Capsule dangers: When climbing in this style you spend a great deal of time jumaring up and rapping down your fixed ropes, so you need to be good with this, and stick to good systems at transitions; you must not get lazy. When you join ropes together, try to do so at solid belays and always, and I mean always, tie off any loose ends with a figure 8 (tie ropes together by using an alpine butterfly knot with a 30 cm tail, then feed the other ropes through the knot to create one knot formed by two ropes, as this is easy to untie and gives you a knot to clip into when you pass it). Never leave a long tail on any joining ropes as many people have been killed or injured by clipping this end instead of the real rope by accident and rapping off it!

When fixing your camp, always try and find a sheltered spot; if there is any chance of loose rock (there is always loose rock!), then you need to keep your camp out of the firing line, or at least pull the ledge up and clip it flat to the wall when no one's home.

02 SPEED CLIMBING

Solo speed climbing is perhaps one of the most difficult forms of climbing one could ever do, up there with winter Himalayan climbing in terms of seriousness. Roped soloing, by its very nature is slow, while one day ascents of walls require the ultimate in fitness, technical skill and strategy. Trying to combine the two (a solo oneday ascent) pushes every single facet of a climber to the very brink

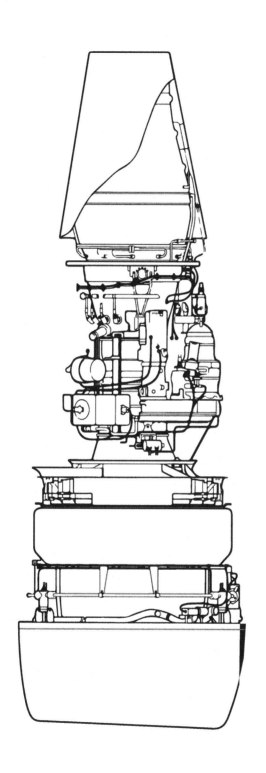

WHY SPEED SOLO?

This is a good question to ask yourself and as with a normal solo ascent, it will be one you will ask many times while trying to pull off such an ascent. Normal roped solos of walls allow the soloist to take their time, free of partners and time constraints; speed soloing, in contrast, is climbing with the clock ticking. Worse than a ticking clock is the level of commitment required. You will be up on the wall, virtually naked, with very little food, water, perhaps totally committed, with no way but up.

So what are the reasons for attempting such a thing? Well, for myself, I find that sense of freedom, climbing with the bare minimum on some huge wall, super exciting … and scary. Approaching a wall like the Leaning Tower with just a 40 litre pack and a rope strapped to the top also makes a change! I like the fact that I have to maintain the highest degree of concentration over such a long period, getting a thrill as I think about doing routes that may take a normal team three or four days and only taking one.

Soloing big walls is something that will only feel right for a small percentage of climbers, perhaps as few as 5%, while speed-soloing will only appeal to 5% of those climbers. Many who try and do a speed ascent will give in within a pitch or so (seeing that the speed needed is just impossible), while some will get to the top, but not in a day. If you persevere and find something addictive in this style of soloing, then like soloing itself, there are great rewards to be had (as well as levels of fatigue, doubt and commitment, it's impossible to quantify unless you've been there, 24 hours in, awake for two days straight with four pitches to go).

The nature of speed
First off, let's get something straight ... solo speed ascents are not just about climbing a wall in a sub-24-hour time. This is the ideal (well the ideal is actually soloing two or three walls in 24 hours!), but really it is the act of soloing a wall as quickly as

possible, which generally means climbing from the bottom to the top without stopping (a push ascent). With any solo speed ascent you should ignore any thoughts of being the fastest or breaking records, just focus on doing it as safely as possible. It's good to know how fast or slow you've been however, so try keep tabs on start and finish times (people are often so wasted at the top they neglect to see when they top out).

Strategy and tactics

What route? You first need to pick a route that will work for a speed ascent, probably one with very few parties to pass, and one that you've climbed several times before. This is one aspect of speed climbing people often don't realise, in that it's very rare for any speed climb to be on-sight, with some impressive teams having climbed the route 10 times or more. If you want to speed solo a route like the Nose, then you'll probably want to have climbed it over a few days beforehand, then half a dozen one day ascents, getting the time down to sub-10 hours.

I know that this may sound a little like loading the dice in your favour, but I can't stress how tough it will be to solo these routes in a day even with this knowledge.

Timing

One of the most important aspects of strategy is when you start, as this will have a big impact on psyche and fatigue. Here are a few ideas:

Pre-sunset: With this you begin before it gets dark, usually as soon as the sun leaves the wall, around 19:00. You then climb all the way through the night and into the next day, the goal to summit before the sun sets again.

Pros: By starting in the dark you eventually climb into the light, which tends to be much easier on your psyche than starting in the morning, with darkness hitting you half way through your speed ascent (darkness + maximum fatigue vs. daylight + maximum fatigue). Also, climbing in the dark at the bottom of the route reduces the amount of water you need, as the bottom of the wall is the hottest part and you will get high before the sun appears.

Cons: By far the worst part about this timing is that invariably you've already been awake all day (if you wake up at 07:00, begin climbing at 19:00, and top out 24 hours later, you'll have been awake for around 36 hours). What if you don't make it to the top in 24 hours? When I first tried to solo Zodiac in a day, I ended up taking over 30 hours to solo the route, by the time I got to the top I'd been awake for over 40 hours ... not good when you're trying to keep your mind focused on climbing.

Alpine start: This is the classic start for most long days, kicking off between 03:00 and 04:00, allowing you to get some sleep before you start (an early night means you can easily get six good hours). For a 24-hour ascent you will climb into the night and your ability not to wilt will only come from experience (the more speed ascents you do, the better you're able to

cope with a lack of sleep and the effects of the night). It's worth trying to make your sleep before the climb as good as possible. Lying on the ground with a scrap of mat under your bum with a shell thrown over you is not conducive to either sleep or rest (you often end up just getting up and starting at 01:00 or bailing before you even begin). Take a good mat, sleeping bag, earplugs, food and brew stuff (you can leave these at the base), so you have the highest chance of being rested before starting.

Pros: You get a night of sleep and so start fresh.

Cons: You will end up climbing in the dark at the end of the day when you're most tired.

Whatever style you use make sure you are 100% rested before you begin.

What rack to take?
On a speed ascent you need to strip everything down to the absolute basics, ideally having only the pieces you need for the route, every cam, nut and

quickdraw there on your rack for a reason. By pre-climbing routes you can note what gear you use and then make a rack based on that accent (it's worth taking a notebook and pen to write down the gear you used on each pitch). You should already have experience in speed climbing with partners, so you will know that back cleaning is a vital part of the speed game, meaning you can further reduce your rack. On most speed climbs I make up two speed rack loops that live on my aiders for the whole route, comprising one rivet hanger, one cam hook, one hook and green, yellow and red aliens (tied to a loop of 7 mm cord), allowing me to just jug up cracks, leaving only gear as protection as I go (again kept to a minimum).

What extra kit to take?
Although you're trying to keep everything down in weight there are a few things you need to take:

• **Pack/haul bag:** You will need somewhere to store all the kit you have (unless you're going super fast) and a medium-sized pack or haul bag works best. Try and get something you can jug with on your back as well as haul, and attach both a clip-off leash and fifi hook to it, so you can quickly set it up for hauling.

• **Head torches:** Light is something you need on a speed ascent, and as head torches can get broken or fall off helmets, always carry a spare with free batteries and fresh batteries for the main head torch (gaffer tape them together in the correct orientation so you can just plug them into your head torch). If your climb necessitates free climbing in the dark, then sticking two small head torches on your ankles (something like a Petzl Tikka) makes it easier to see what you're standing on.

• **Warm clothing:** If you're climbing through the night you need something warm to wear (it can get very cold even on a wall, even in the summer). A light, hooded, synthetic top works well, as it packs down small, will work wet or dry and is windproof. Add a thin balaclava as well.

• **Shell:** You should have a very light shell and trousers (keep an eye on the forecast).

• **Micro mat:** A super thin mat (the type you find in backpacks) is worth having, as you can sleep on it on a ledge if need be, or at the top.

• **Knife:** Ropes get stuck and might need cutting, plus abseil tat could need cutting out of pegs, so a knife is a good thing to have.

• **Lighter:** When you top out you may need to make a fire to stay warm, so having a small lighter is handy.

Food and water: You need to be well fuelled with before you start, so it's worth loading up on pasta the day before, as well as being well hydrated (taking a stove to the bottom allows you to eat some porridge and have a brew as you rack up). On the climb, ideally, you should eat something before each pitch (such as a power gel or a quarter of a power bar), maintaining your fluid intake as you go. Often when you're climbing really fast you can ignore eating and drinking, then all of a sudden you bonk (generally high on the wall, when you really don't want to be bonking), so try to keep taking on food and water regularly. I also take some real food with me, like a big sandwich, which I'll eat at designated spots such as good ledges, allowing me to take stock.

Water – this is the killer. Water is heavy and will slow you down, while without it you'll soon fade. By starting in the night you reduce the need for water, but once the sun shines you will wilt without it (it's vital to stay covered up as well, plus wear light clothing). Having 3 litres per day is the norm for a wall, but seeing as you'll be climbing for longer, I'd say 6 litres is the minimum for a speed ascent. This will add quite a bit of weight to your pack or haul bag, but I think this weight will translate into more efficient (and safer) climbing. In the past I've always used a bladder when climbing, but I can see that those extra kilos on my back were probably not worth the luxury of sipping every few minutes, and so I've gone back to having the water in bottles at the belay.

One small tip is to avoid drinking every drop of water you have and always have at least one mouthful left when you reach the top. Once that last drop has gone your thirst will be twice as bad as just knowing it's still in your bottle.

Don't forget to take plenty of energy powder and electrolytes as well.

Stashing water: One aspect of speed climbing that is never discussed is the amount of water that is stashed on walls before the event. It's not uncommon to come across bottles hidden in cracks or on ledges with labels asking for the water not to be drunk until after X date. Having 3 litres of water stashed three quarters of the way up a wall gives you something to aim for, but in my mind it's kind of cheating and sort of undermines what you're trying to do (to be independent and alone on a big wall). Also, what happens if you just set off with 1 litre in your bladder pack and you get to your stash point only to find that the water has gone?

Micro naps: Sleeping on a speed ascent may sound counterproductive, but if you're totally done in then it may be a necessity. Taking a 15 minute sleep every 4 hours will improve your ability to operate while still climbing (this is based on studies of soldiers in combat, who may be forced to fight without sleep for days on end). If you have a sleep then don't go over 15–30 minutes, as you will go into REM sleep and will feel dreadful when you wake up. If you're really tired, then sleeping may become involuntary (I've experienced many bouts of micro napping, when you just wake up and realise that you were asleep, which is a bit scary when you're on a wall all alone!).

Passing parties: If you reach a party on a wall and you're alone, you really can't wait for them to finish as they're probably going to be up there for days! You should try and communicate with them before you reach them and tell them what you're doing (they may hold off leading the next pitch). If the leader is already half way up the next pitch you can either: (a) begin climbing up and pass them on the pitch (not ideal); (b) ask if you can just jug the haul line when the leader reaches the belay (spoils your solo ascent but is fast and gets you past them); or (c) solo the pitch on the gear already there (you use it as fixed gear). The ideal is to get the route without any parties on it, or time it so that the parties are all in bed (waking people up at 03:00 is always a bit tricky, but then it's a big wall and that's the kind of crazy stuff you sign up for).

Rope or ropes: On a speed ascent you need to use a long, light, single rope (anything from a 9 mm to 10 mm single, with a 70 or 80 metre rope being ideal). A long rope will allow you to string two or even three pitches together (remember that when rope soloing you have no rope drag). Setting up belays and cleaning takes time,

so by removing several belays on a route you save a lot of time. On my first go at soloing the Leaning Tower in a day, I free-aid soloed up the first set of bolts (free-aid soloing is soloing without a rope, just trusting the gear), and then managed to link four pitches with one 80 metre rope (only just), saving a huge amount of time.

Another factor to consider is: do you bring a second rope? A second rope can be used both for rapping down from the belay to clean the pitch and haul (as in the normal solo technique), as well as retreating (an 80 metre rope is usually long enough to double up on most classic walls, as pitches tend to be short). The downside being that another rope is another rope, and adds more work to the climbing. If you can carry your bag on your back when cleaning, you save time used in hauling, and if you can just rappel down the lead rope, then you won't need that second one. The problem, however, is that rapping a lead rope on a steep wall can be very tricky, especially if the pitch traverses (again it comes down to knowing the route).

SPEED TECHNIQUES

A lot of speed climbing just relies on the same techniques used in a normal ascent, but below are a couple of techniques that are handy to know.

Free-aid solo: This technique is basically ropeless aid soloing, just trusting the gear you're on (which is invariably a single cam or bolt), and it has been used a lot for speed soloing walls that feature long sections of uniform cracks (such as the Nose). To utilise this technique you should attach the gear directly to your daisy chain via a locker; you need to be 100% sure it's solid (both the gear and the rock) before taking out the last piece. You can increase your safety by using a third daisy chain, so you always have two pieces in at all times. Whatever system you use, it comes down to experience, as an experienced climber knows that a well-placed cam is pretty much as good as a belay (when you're 500 metres up on a wall you may think differently). When free-aid soloing you need to do something with your rope, so you can either stick it on your back or trail it (clip into it at the halfway mark, so you don't have a huge strand hanging down). If you're using a haul bag or pack, then this can be attached to the end of the rope and hung from an attached fifi hook. Upon reaching the belay you can pull up the pack via the fifi.

Death loop: The death loop is a high risk technique used in order to avoid having to rap and clean a pitch, but at the expense of any real degree of safety. The best way to imagine this system is as a reversed retrievable rap. Instead of going down and pulling your ropes, you are going to be going up and pulling your ropes.

To do a death loop the climber:

1. Places a leaver biner on one bolt, either a locker, maillon or tapedshut non-locker.

2. They then pass one end of the rope through the anchor krab and tie this into their harness.

3. Once the other side of the

rope, they attach their self-belay device (Silent Partner/GriGri) and clip this to their harness.

4. They now tie a backup knot several metres further along the rope.

5. The rest of the rope will either need to just hang in space (for this reason the death loop works best with very thin ropes), lay on a ledge, or be carried by the leader in a bag.

6. The leader begins to climb, the loop they have formed getting larger as they go. If they only have a single 60 metre rope it will all be used up at 30 metres (for full length pitches climbers may tie two 60 metre ropes together).

7. The soloist can climb without any gear at all depending on their ability not to fall, or they can place gear or clip fixed gear, but this will need to be left behind (you will only be able to clip one or two pieces like this per pitch).

8. Once the soloist has reached the belay or where they wish

to retrieve their rope (you may want to set up a new belay mid pitch from a bolt), they simply untie the end attached to their harness and pull it through (as you would if you were abseiling).
And so they can get some safely without losing time rapping down and cleaning.

The potential forces created in a

fall onto your belay device could be way beyond what would be healthy, so this should be considered as a high-risk system.

Super death loop: An alternative to the death loop is the 'super death loop', which is really only one step up from free-aid soloing. With this system you would not place/clip any gear on the pitch, but instead rely only on leapfrogging your gear without placing any protection (the same technique as free-aid soloing). The basic idea is the same as free-aid soloing except that you clip the rope at its middle mark to the belay bolt (clipping rather than threading saves time), then you either clip into both ends with two lockers into your harness and start climbing (so you have two 30 metre loops below you), or in short (say two 20 metre loops below you, plus two 10 metre rope ends). By removing the 'moving belay' component to reduce the hassle of snagging ropes, knots etc. (plus not placing gear), saves both time and the possibility of the rope hanging up when

pulling through at the end of the pitch. The obvious downside is potentially taking a 60 metre or even 120 metre (if using two ropes tied together) fall, and so this only really works on very steep routes; it is considered close to free soloing, or base jumping without a chute!

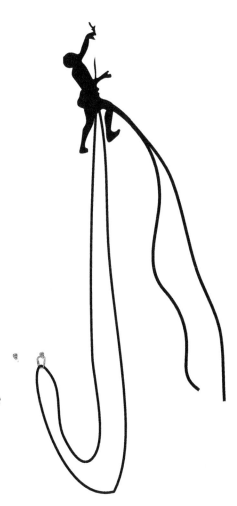

You must take into account the length of rope you have available when undertaking this technique, especially if using only one, as it must be twice as long as any pitch. Some climbers wanting to both use the death loop on and string pitches together will tie two 70 metre ropes together, but personably, adding a knot could be a bad idea and I would opt for an extra-long skinny super long rope (80 or 100 metre). Alternatively, don't be too greedy and just climb pitch to pitch.

Cleaning pitches on a single rope: If you're speed climbing on a single rope then you will have to rap the rope back to the belay to clean. When leading, have in mind that you'll be coming back down the pitch, avoiding any acute angle changes in the rope, aiming instead to have the rope running in as straight a line as possible. Using 60 cm and 120 cm slings can help reduce these acute deviations and long quickdraws are recommended.

Before you begin to rap it's worth setting up a prusik on your belay device (a GriGri is better, and highly recommended for cleaning such pitches), as well as maybe running the rope over two lockers (to give you more control on a skinny single rope). Have one daisy chain/ aider ready to clip into the gear as you go down. Start rapping, and when you reach each piece of protection, just switch it over your descender device. If the angle gets steep you will find that you will not be able to unclip the gear to pass the device, as it will be overloaded. Just clip in your aider and step into it, taking your weight off the rope, allowing you to pass the protection. Now re-weight the descender, unclip your aider and keep on going. Unless it seems like a really good idea, avoid cleaning gear on your way down, as it will invariably make it harder to jug up (especially on steep walls), plus, it just adds more unnecessary weight when jugging (having the rope running through gear reduces the edge abrasion on a skinny rope too). If you find yourself in space and unable to reach the gear, you may need to jug or pull yourself into the gear and, again, use your aider to pass it.

Retreating up or down? You need to have a solid understanding of both the climb and yourself when on a solo speed climb. Bonk or run out of steam/water 15 pitches up with the sun about to hit you, and you will be well a truly knackered! Don't climb into such a predicament, as you will either end up having to be rescued, or you will be so out of it you will probably kill yourself (once your water is gone, your difficulties/fatigue will increase by 50% each hour). Knowing well before you reach exhaustion that it's time to turn around should give you a greater chance of making it down safely. At the same time, perhaps you're so high you know that going up is the only option? In this case try and plan out an upward escape in order to give you the best chances of pulling it off. Can you hitch a ledge and get 15 minutes' sleep? How about reducing your pace? As I've said, being alone in the dark, high on a wall with only a scrap of food and a mouthful of water, is one of the most committing things you will ever do.

Getting to the top: When you get to the top of the wall you will probably be more exhausted than you thought possible, and will instantly want to drop to the ground and sleep for a week. Unless you have the opportunity to sleep for several hours, try and avoid sleeping more than 40 minutes; instead, have a micro nap then start on down. Once down, be very careful if driving any distance! The toll of a solo speed ascent on your body and mind is considerable and it could take many weeks to get back to normal again (sometimes the very idea of being up on a wall alone again repulsive). It's for this reason that you should plan your attempt carefully, as you really only get one shot.

03 LOOKING AFTER #1

The main use for your first aid kit is for patching yourself up so you can keep going, while your ability to deal with a major trauma will be limited. In most cases, if something serious happens then you will need to get yourself to a point where you can stabilise yourself and wait for rescue. Your ability to deal with a major incident in a remote wilderness situation is of the utmost importance; failing to manage this could well be a death sentence unless you can get word out for a rescue to come to your aid.

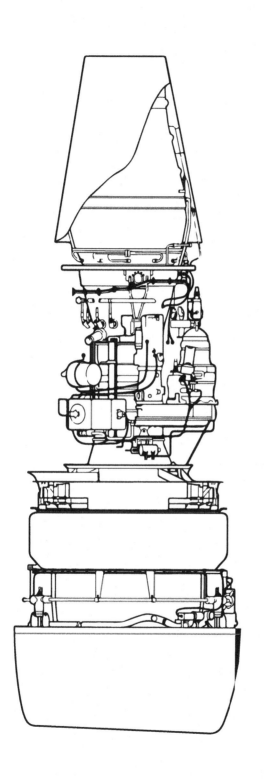

This is one reason why soloing walls in Yosemite or the Alps is a good idea, as there is always someone looking out for you, and rescue can be very swift indeed. Robert Steiner had one of his fingers cut off in a fall on the Sea of Dreams on El Cap, but managed to get himself down and to a hospital; a broken leg or arm would make retreat almost impossible on anything but the easiest of walls, while a broken pelvis would make it impossible to get down.

First Aid Kit
The parts of you that will get the most hammered are your hands and fingers, followed by your feet, then your skin (either sunburn in the summer or frost-nip in the winter), so your first aid kit should reflect this.

Hands: It's vital that you look after any cuts and abrasions on your hands, as infections will develop quickly on a wall, especially one that has a lot of human waste on it. Cover cuts with strappel after cleaning them and replace the tape when it gets ratty. If you're wearing

gloves then your hands should be fine (save for the odd hot spot). One reason I tend to wear full length leather gloves is that it's the fingers that get the most wear and tear (remember that on a wall you're doing way more than three times the work, so your hands must absorb three times more punishment).

It's always worth carrying a little tube of hand cleaner to use at the end of the day before eating, or after having a crap, plus some hand cream to stop them cracking (Vitamin E balms designed for bouldering work well, as they can be bought in tiny pots, otherwise Nivea works fine).

So look after your hands!

Feet: Your feet can get really hammered if you have soft shoes, leaving both your toes and arches (were your aiders run around your foot) in agony. There is not much you can do about this once you're on the wall, and can only really be avoided by wearing stiff boots with plenty of room for your toes. Wearing sweaty boots for days on end can lead to athlete's foot, so it's vital to wear clean, dry, socks, while aiming to keep your feet dry. Use talc or fungal powder at night after cleaning with a wet wipe. I find that tea tree oil works well on the feet as well as other cuts in general. Like your fingers, if your skin begins to wear, then tape up the area.

Basic extras: Beyond these items it's worth having some of the following first aid essentials: paracetamol and ibuprofen (take both for severe pain); co-codamol (be aware this will make you tired and affect your ability to deal with problems if you're already wasted); safety pins, scalpel and a paperclip (if you smash your finger and get blood under the nail, which is agony, you heat up end of the paperclip and pierce your nail to release the pressure); iodine and some dressings, as well as the usual stuff you tend to get in a first aid kit. Keep in mind, Dioralyte is an absolute must on hot walls like El Cap.

Oh shit! first aid: If you're in a wilderness setting or on a wall that's hard to rescue from, a major accident will leave your life in the hands of the gods, but even then, there may be some things you can do to give them (and your rescuers) some extra time to save your ass. This can be split into injury stabilisation and pain management. Having a good clotting agent such as Quikclot, plus a number of large dressings and bandages, could help to reduce blood loss, and using other items such as a sleeping mat and gaffer tape will do the rest. For pain relief you should not take anything super strong as you need to be able to deal with the situation, but in a wilderness situation you should have super strong pain meds at your basecamp, as you may be forced to wait a long time for a rescue; in the short term, adrenaline should see you through.

Serious injury: The German soloist Robert Steiner lost a finger while trying to solo The Sea of Dreams on El Cap, but managed to get down and to a hospital. If you break a leg, hip or arm, you will be rendered helpless and your life will probably depend on getting rescued, so some form of communication is vital. These injuries may spoil your day but, unseen injuries can be more deadly, with blunt trauma to the body resulting in internal bleeding a real killer.

Insurance: Perhaps the most important part of your emergency kit is your rescue insurance, as just about every wall you'd want to solo lies in an area where you'll be charged for a rescue. In some places charging depends on whether the rescuers feel you were ill prepared, foolhardy or negligent, so make sure you're none of the above and have insurance as a backup. On any wall make sure you have all your documents, passport and credit cards where they can be easily grabbed in a rescue (many teams will not risk their lives to rescue your kit). If you find yourself in hospital without ID or a credit card, there is a chance they may let you die (I know of someone who was refused a rescue helicopter unless he could produce a credit card). For an example of costs I talked to someone who was rescued one pitch up El Cap. The rescue team carried him on a stretcher no more than 500 metres to a helicopter for a ride to hospital. He was fine in the end, but his final bill was $19,000 (enough to bankrupt him).

Beyond the initial rescue, the real costs come from hospital bills and repatriation. You do not want to find yourself without insurance in these situations, unless you're planning on just dragging your broken body onto a plane to get home (this actually happens … one partner I had broke her leg once and waited a week until she flew home to get it sorted!).

When buying insurance make sure you're totally clear on what you're doing and get written confirmation they understand you're soloing, as any policy is void if you're not covered in the small print. At the moment the best insurance schemes seem to be provided by the British Mountaineering Council, The

American Alpine Club and The French Alpine Club. Make sure you pay close attention to how much cover you get on medical bills, as some only cover rescue. An case in point of cheap insurance is that of the Austrian Alpine Club (a cheap provider that all skinflint climbers recommend). Some friends of mine had one of their team die on an expedition and upon ringing the emergency number for the Austrian Alpine Club on their satellite phone, they could only reach someone who spoke no English!

Rescue

If you're climbing in Yosemite or on a wall in a popular spot with plenty of traffic, then people will notice if you get into trouble. A rescue team will generally make contact via a loudspeaker to check how you are, and then if they decide you need rescuing, they will communicate how they will rescue you (most walls are too steep for long line helicopter rescues, so a rescuer is usually lowered from the summit). Even so, you should always try and have someone on the ground

looking out for you, someone who has an idea when you're meant to be getting off the wall. Leaving a card in your car or tent with a phone number, your name and the routes you plan on climbing (plus next of kin), can make things easier; you could even just pop in and tell the mountain rescue guys what you're up to.

If you get into trouble on a wilderness wall, you're in the shit. Before committing to a wall, you need to ask yourself these questions:

• Could I be rescued if I get into trouble?

• Who would come to rescue me?

• How could I tell them I need rescuing?

The only way you really have a fighting chance (unless you're going to drag your broken body back to civilisation) is by way of an Emergency Position Indicating Radio Beacon (EPIRB) (there are many brands, with SPOT being the most common for outdoors pursuits) or a satellite phone. Nonetheless, even with these fancy gadgets, you need to understand that when you need rescuing, the weather or darkness will invariably be against you.

The bottom line is don't fall.

04 PHOTOGRAPHY

One question I get asked a lot from people who see slideshows of solo climbs is: "How did you take so many photos?" The answer is generally "with great difficulty", as soloing a wall is just about the toughest multi-tasking challenge a climber could ever do, and adding in the chore of documenting it is just one thing extra to think about. And yet, although taking photos or filming can feel like absolutely the last thing you want to do, you need to think of the future and make that effort.

Have a record of what could well be the greatest experience of your life will provide you with a way of revisiting your finest hour (finest week probably), and looking at what you did years later is like watching a total stranger doing something you'd never consider doing. Documenting it will allow you to write or talk about it and share the experience (people are fascinated by such journeys into the unknown parts of the human psyche).

The plan

Before you set out on your climb, spend a little while making a plan of what you would like to have 'in the can' at the end of your climb. You need to have a shopping list of shots, movies or audio written down in your notebook, as well as a storyboard of images.

These lists should allow you to take your audience on a journey, from the very start of the climb, through the highs and lows, to the summit (or the not-summit, which in many ways is a greater story). Have a look at what others have done, what shots they got, how they talked about their climb, see if they have a story with a start, middle and end.

Here is a suggested shot list sequence (try and get both stills and video, talking directly to the camera as you film):

• Packing your bags;

• Your rack (what everything does);

• Film yourself talking out the trip (include doubts and fears);

• Arriving at the airport;Check in;

• On the plane;

• Travelling with bags;

• First site of the climb;

• First moves;

• First haul;

• First bivy etc.

The video diary doc

When ticking off your shot list, aim to produce a video diary of the trip. Do this by getting into a routine of filming yourself talking in the morning and at night, as well as when you feel you need to share something with others. This routine will help you produce a lot of interesting footage (you won't know its value until months or years later), but more importantly in the short term, you may not feel quite so alone, as you will be speaking directly to your future self (as well as your audience).

Equipment

In the past there was a huge amount of faff and expense with solo filming, using SLRs with infrared remotes and limited ability to get the correct shot (36 shots versus tens of thousands with a large capacity SD card). These days we have small and medium compact cameras that can capture film and stills that fit in a pocket and can be fired with cheap remotes; then there's God's gift to solo filmmakers and photographers

... the GoPro. An alternative to this would be to use a modern smartphone, which would allow you to do all these things as well as upload your media direct to websites (as long as you have phone coverage). In reality, most climbers will use a combination of all three to achieve a good mix of media and outcomes from it (YouTube/Vimeo videos, slideshows, magazine articles etc.).

On a typical solo climb I will carry a small compact camera (generally Canon) with three batteries, carrying it in a case on my harness (I use as small a LowePro case as I can find and attach the camera to it with a 3 mm bungee; the case is always attached via its loop and backed up with a small krab clipped to a gear rack). When choosing a camera, get one that has HD video, sound and some macro ability. I tend to glue a small patch of pile on my camera's mic to add some wind-noise resistance.

The second camera I carry is a GoPro (I'm using a GoPro 3 at the moment) mounted on a medium-sized Gorillapod. I carry spare SD cards and batteries for this, as it's very easy to forget about it when filming, and fill both a card and drain a battery. I tend to use the open-backed case for my GoPro in order to get better sound quality. I also make a small modification to the case by gluing on some velcro for attaching a small bottle top so as to stop the camera switching on by accident (the number one reason for battery draining).

The Gorillapod is modified to be used on the wall by adding a clip-in loop made from 2 mm cord that loops mid-way up one leg and then carries on up and wraps around the tripod mount. The mount should be super-glued to the GoPro mount (you can remove the mount from the GoPro and slip on a different mount, but the tripod/GoPro mount is fixed). This clip in loop works well as a lanyard for the camera (so it can't be lost), but also as an attachment point for securing it to protection, so as to get interesting shots. To use this feature all you need to do is fix it to some protection, a belay or even your rope via a prusik, then down climb a short way and get your shots.

The GoPro can be attached via your helmet or GoPro head strap, you can also add a mount to a Petzl head-torch strap to get double duty from it. These point-of-view shots can be good but if overused, can prove very boring (the 'death by powerpoint' of film making). It is better to mix up the shots and use more direct to camera footage, with the odd POV shot thrown in here and there.

Another useful accessory in the GoPro stick, either a GoPro model or a ski pole (the GoPro model is probably best, as it's set up already). With this and the camera set on wide angle, you can get some great shots on a wall but, again, don't overdo it, as your final video will be dull (your audience will soon tire of 'amazing' shots of you holding a stick over a big drop). One of the most effective uses of a GoPro for solo photography is the auto sequence shooting mode, where the camera takes a photo every few seconds.

This works very well when hauling, leading, sitting on a bivy (in fact anywhere you're doing something and want to just let the camera run). When using this feature make sure you turn off the GoPro after a minute, otherwise you'll end up with several thousand shots (setting the GoPro to switch off automatically after four minutes is a very good idea).

A great add-on for the GoPro is the bluetooth remote; it not only allows you to switch the camera on or off from medium distances (and so gets shots of you on lead), but it also allows you to see what you're shooting via a smartphone running the GoPro app (something undreamt off only ten years ago).

If you plan on filming everything, then you should consider using more than one GoPro, so you can leave them below filming, with spares ready to set up higher (filming on traverses always works very well).

THE BASICS

Macro to micro: Many photographers and novice filmmakers focus too much on the 'big picture', the nice views, the big drops, the action, and not so much on the tiny things that make up that world (the moss of a tree, worn fingertips, a battered cam lobe). Mixing the two, macro and micro, helps to create a fuller picture of the climb and the experience, and although it might be just me, I tend to remember these small things more than the views.

Capture the fundamentals: When filming your climb, imagine you need to provide footage to someone who's never climbed before, to show them them how each part of your solo is carried out. Take hauling for example, you could just set up your GoPro and have 10 minutes of you hauling, but that would be deadly dull. Instead, get 2 minutes of you hauling, then get some cutaways and close-ups of: setting up the pulley, the rope running through the pulley, pulling the rope, and tying off the haul bag etc. Try and film one aspect well each day (bivying, cleaning, hauling, leading, having a crap etc.), so that when you add it to your diary footage, stills and other stuff, you'll have a complete picture.

The BIG reveal: One type of shot that always works well in slideshows is the 'big reveal'. You begin by focusing up close to something (a piece of protection, the belay, your face talking), then pan upwards to show where you need to get to, then very slowly pan back down to show the wall underneath. This will invariably get an "oooh!" out of the audience.

People please: I often joke that climbing is like 'masturbation', its fun doing it, but people aren't that interested in hearing about it, and I stand by that. If it was just the act of moving over stone, we'd soon get bored and switch off. What keeps our attention is the personal journey, the struggle, the backstory, how this person can keep going against the odds. Focusing on the climbing, perhaps to show how hard it is,

is a very common mistake in all climbing-related media, and it invariably falls flat. Fear or doubt is universal and it makes no difference the size of the holds. Instead of the grade, focus on the human story. Be bold and speak the truth about how you feel each day, be honest, and people will understand you and follow your story.

Social media: If Captain Scott or Roald Amundsen had had access to Facebook, Twitter and Instagram, they would have used these to their full potential, but only having pen and paper, they wrote diaries instead, their words ready to be shared via the social media of the 1900s (books and newspapers). Climbers in the twenty-first century can employ previously undreamt-of technology to fully document their whole climbing experience using nothing but their phone, capturing video, stills and audio, as well as stringing together oldschool words to write a description of their experience, all of which can then be upload to social media sites or personal websites in an instant (well as long as you have a phone connection).

I've attempted to do this on several climbs, including tough alpine walls on the Eiger and Troll (where I took an iPad!) with varying degrees of success. On my near solo ascent of the Troll wall I wrote and posted a blog every night (which was no mean feat), and although some people probably thought I was just blowing my own trumpet, I found this aspect of the challenge as interesting as the climb.

A good smart phone should be able to do all you need in terms of a 'one stop shop' for a wall, and as discussed above, could perhaps replace both your camera and GoPro, allowing you to upload content directly. In more remote areas, where it's hard to upload big files, then having some way of reducing file sizes of images is vital. On the Troll Wall I uploaded directly to my own blog, but having someone at the end of an email to sort out your content could be easier.

When picking a smartphone try and see which ones offer a case that will protect it as well as allow it to remain secure (some kind of clip-in loop). Also check out the availability of accessories such as a tripod mount as well as apps (photo editing, text editing, ftp and file shrinking) before buying. One big thing for me is battery power and this is one thing where Samsung phones win over Apple, as iPhones have a fixed battery, while Samsung phones allow the battery to be switched out for a new one. If you're using a fixed-battery smartphone (or iPad) then you will need to carry a separate battery/ power source.

{ Endnote }

So you've come to the end of this book. How do you feel? Excited maybe, perhaps the opposite, your dreams of soloing El Cap dashed by the reality of its seriousness and complexity. Maybe you had never considered this kind of quest before, but now you do. My advice would be don't rush into anything, let that dream simmer, let the good and the bad imaginings of how and what it could be stew. If you find your big wall daydreams growing, then go with it. Learn and practise the skills you'll need, read other books, immerse yourself with the lore and legend of soloing. And then perhaps one day you will find yourself waking to a full moon, shining down like the torch of a ranger, startling you, making your forget where you are. And then you'll feel the space beneath you, your sore hands aching, the hard granite beneath your mat and you'll remember.

And you'll never forget

Lightning Source UK Ltd.
Milton Keynes UK
UKOW01f0033090218
317587UK00005B/295/P

A SUSSEX QUIZ BOOK

Testing your knowledge of town and country,
history and geography, yesterday and today.

David Arsc(

Illustrated by Geoffre

S.B. Publications

By the same author:

The Sussex Story
Curiosities of East Sussex
Curiosities of West Sussex
Hastings and The 1066 Country
The Upstart Gardener

Co-author (with Warden Swinfen)

Hidden Sussex
People of Hidden Sussex
Hidden Sussex Day by Day
Hidden Sussex - the Towns

First published in 1993 by S.B. Publications.
c/o 19 Grove Road, Seaford, East Sussex BN25 1TP

ISBN 1 85770 028 7

Typeset and printed by Island Press Ltd.,
3 Cradle Hill Industrial Estate, Seaford, East Sussex BN25 3JE.
Telephone: (0323) 490222

CONTENTS

Front cover photograph: who had this pyramid built, and why?
Back cover: which castle is this, and where was the picture taken?
(Answers on p.64)

INTRODUCTION

There is no companion more unbearable than the know-all, and a book which sets out to tease your brain while having every relevant fact neatly stored at the back as evidence against you seems destined to be flung into the furthest corner of the room with as wild an oath as you can bring yourself to utter. If you manage to overcome this understandable temptation it can only be because the teasing is enjoyable, and I have therefore devised a few simple stratagems which I hope will work the trick. They can be summarised as follows:

— no outlandishly obscure questions of the kind: *Who said of Pevensey Marshes 'How sweet they are to tread in summer!'?* If anyone *did* say such a thing there's no good reason why you, or I, should know it.

— no vague open-ended questions of the kind: *Where will you find one of the best examples of a Norman chancel arch?* Lazy compilers devise such horrors by flicking through history books and turning simple statements into meaningless questions. There are, of course, several fine Norman chancel arches.

— all questions to seem *worth* the asking, in that their subject matter is interesting.

— all questions to be posed in such a fashion that the answer, if not known, can be entertainingly guessed. Far better to ask *'How did Michael Turner die?'* than the much tougher *'Who died playing the violin?'* (At Horsham in 1885, and the question *doesn't* appear in the book).

The danger of setting out these rules so clearly is that I shall inevitably be taken to task for breaking them in this or that instance, but there is at the least an impetus in favour of both fairness and fun.

As to difficulty, there is no grading system to make one set of questions intentionally more demanding than another; nor is there any progression within the individual rounds themselves. This means that questions can be chosen at random should you be using the book for family or group competitions.

Since one-word answers can be infuriating, I have attempted to flesh out the basic details with a little extra information where this seems desirable. For further reading I am happy, for obvious reasons, thoroughly to recommend the books listed on an earlier page.

David Arscott

1. SUSSEX BOOK OF RECORDS

With its softly rolling Downs and its richly wooded Weald, Sussex is the gentlest and most undemonstrative of counties. We begin, nevertheless, with a round of extremes.

1. It's been described as the largest representation of the human form anywhere in the world. What is it?

2. The heaviest hailstone ever recorded in Britain fell on Horsham on September 5, 1958. How much did it weigh?

3. When the very last specimen died in Sussex in 1992, this became the first species of mammal to become extinct in Britain since the wolf in 1740. What was it?

4. Allowing for the cross on top, Sussex can lay claim to the tallest parish church in England. Which is it?

5. Who was the first man to be killed in a railway accident?

Where will you find:

6. The highest point in Sussex?

7. The longest tithe barn?

8. The smallest house?

9. The smallest port?

10. The smallest church?

hAROLD

2. FAMOUS MEN

AD 477. This year came Aella to Britain, with his three sons, Clymen and Wlenking and Cissa, in three ships; landing at a place that is called Clymenshore.

(An excerpt from The Anglo Saxon Chronicle, from which it's generally inferred that Aella was the first king of the South Saxons - or Sussex. Rather more is known about the following)

1. Charles Wells, who lived at no 86 Fort Road in Newhaven in 1891, was later immortalised in song. What is he known as?

2. Archie Belaney was a Hastings Grammar School boy who travelled and changed his name. To what?

3. His Christian names were Johann Heinrich, and he gave his name to a famous training centre in East Sussex.

4. The London hatter Sir Richard Hotham hoped that a West Sussex resort would be named after him. It wasn't. What do we call the place today?

5. William Robinson lived at Gravetye Manor, near East Grinstead. What was his field of expertise?

6. Canon Nathaniel Woodard, who lived at Henfield, founded three famous colleges. Name them.

7. What service did Sake Deen Mahomed provide for George IV, formerly the Prince Regent?

8. The ashes of Karl Marx's friend and collaborator Friedrich Engels were scattered in Sussex after his death in 1895. Where?

9. Whom did Nicholas Tettersell save?

10. Charles Goring planted a Sussex landmark in 1760. What is it?

3. THE ARTS

'The studio... was half work-room and half sitting-room, redolent of oil and turpentine. Easels and paintboxes stood about, brushes, sometimes festooned with cobwebs, emerged from jugs or jam jars, palettes and tubes of paint lay on stools or tables, while there was often a bunch of red-hot pokers and dahlias arranged in front of a piece of drapery.'

(Angelica Garnett on living among artists at Charleston farmhouse in Sussex)

1. John Christie founded it, as a stage for his wife.

2. He lived at Rottingdean for many years, designed three stained-glass windows in the church and is buried there.

3. This famous composer travelled through Sussex collecting old folk songs.

4. Many members of the Broadwood family are buried at Rusper. What are they known for?

5. A famous ballet dancer who spent his last months at Rustington.

6. Another Rustington resident: this one set Blake's *Jerusalem* to music.

7. She was a member of the Bloomsbury set and painted the walls of a Sussex church.

8. Two would-be ostriches stand outside Pallant House, Chichester's art gallery. What do locals call the building?

9. John Wesley Woodward was a cellist with several orchestras in the Eastbourne area. Where did he give his last performance?

10. Among this artist's Sussex works are painting of deer and sunsets in Petworth Park.

4. CASTLES & OTHER DEFENCES

Lo! where yon Ruin stands! the poor remains
Of what in former times adorn'd the scene;
The Muse from history this knowledge gains,
That great in former ages it has been...

(Lady Burrell on Knepp Castle, 1788)

1. Which Sussex castle has two mottes?

2. Seaford's was no. 74 and the last of the chain - of what?

3. During the civil war, Parliamentary troops bombarded this castle from guns mounted on the tower of the parish church nearby.

4. The Normans built it to defend the valley of the river Adur.

5. It was the only Sussex castle built during the reign of Henry VIII.

6. The castle ruins are on the West Hill.

7. From Pett Level into Kent in order to thwart Napoleon. What was it?

8. Wolstonbury, the Trundle, Mount Caburn: what do they have in common?

9. A Roman castle with Norman additions.

10. King John used to visit Knepp Castle, of which only a fragment now remains. By which main road can it be seen?

5. FAMOUS WOMEN

One who never turned her back
　　but marched breast forward,
Never doubted clouds would break,
Never dreamed, though right were
　　worsted, wrong would triumph,
Held we fall to rise, are baffled to
　　fight better,
　　　Sleep to wake.

(Epitaph to Elizabeth Blackwell)

1. She was at the centre of a Victorian political scandal. Her Irish lover's letters were buried beneath her head in Littlehampton cemetery.

2. Martha Gunn was famous in Regency Brighton. What was she?

3. Which institution was founded by Penelope, Dorothy and Millicent Lawrence?

4. Phoebe Hessel is buried in St Nicholas' churchyard, Brighton. What is she known for?

5. Lady Joan Pelham achieved something remarkable for a woman at Pevensey in 1399. What was it?

6. There are plaques in Hastings to Elizabeth Blackwell and Sophia Jex Blake, nineteenth century pioneers. In what field?

7. This bold leader of men narrowly escaped assassination in Sussex.

8. Mrs Adelaide Hoodless founded an organisation which established its first English branch at Singleton and East Dean in 1915. What was it?

9. A vivacious young lady who later became the mistress of an admiral is said to have danced on a table at Uppark House. By what name do we know her?

10. The Ditchling sweetheart.

6. SUSSEX DIALECT

The Rev. William Parish, vicar of Selmeston, published his Dictionary of the Sussex Dialect *in 1875, and these questions are based upon it. It's rare to hear the old Sussex spoken these days, but during my long radio association with Bert Winborne (the hero of my book,* The Upstart Gardener) *I became acquainted with many a word which Parish recorded more than a century earlier.*

1. Most of us have been afflicted by an *ampre-ang* at one time or another. What is it?

2. How do you feel if you're *beazled?*

3. 'Cut your stick!' advised the old man. What did he mean?

4. A *husser-and-squencher* was a mixed alcoholic drink. What were its two components?

5. A pretty flower was known as *jump-up-and-kiss-me.* Which one?

6. If you admit *Old Laurence has got hold of me,* what are you saying about yourself?

7. What did a farmer refer to as a *mawkin?*

8. What's another word for *nunty* behaviour?

9. And what does it mean to be *quotted?*

10. She was *up-a-top-of-the-house.* Meaning what?

7. RELIGIOUS TYPES

And I said to the man who stood at the gate of the year: 'Give me a light, that I may tread safely into the unkown.' And he replied, 'Go out into the darkness and put your hand into the hand of God. That shall be to you better than light and safer than a known way.'

(Lines chosen by George VI for his first wartime Christmas Day broadcast, and written by the unknown Minnie Louise Haskins, who lived at Crowborough)

1. James Hannington from Hurstpierpoint was an Anglican missionary killed by the natives in Eastern Equatorial Africa. A childhood accident had left him with a minor deformity. What was missing?

2. John Mason Neale was warden of Sackville College in East Grinstead until his death in 1866. Which famous Christmas carol did he write?

3. Where did John Wesley preach his last open-air sermon?

4. St Cuthman brought his crippled mother to Steyning: by what manner of transport?

5. St Richard was a miracle-worker. Where's his shrine?

6. In 1655 Thomas Lawcock became the first of his kind to be imprisoned in Sussex. What form of religion did he practise?

7. William Huntingdon, the evangelical preacher, founded the Jireh Chapel at Cliffe, Lewes, in 1805. His gravestone has the letters SS after his name. What do they stand for?

8. The preacher John Sirgood founded the Society of Dependants (commonly known as the Cokelers) in north Sussex in 1850. How had he previously earned his living?

9. Canon Arthur Barwick Simpson, rector of Fittleworth at the end of the nineteenth century, published an account of some pioneering, and influential, research. Into what?

10. A father and son dominated Brighton's religious life from 1824 until 1902. They built churches, founded charities and became involved in bitter High Church controversies. What was their surname?

8. MISCELLANEOUS

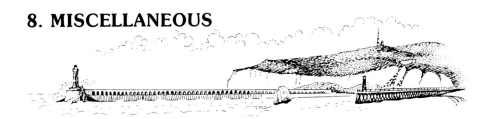

A round for which you need to know little more than folklore, Old English, geology, Roman and Norman history, maritime matters and the penal system.

1. James Burton had a dream one night of building a beautiful town by the sea - and he acted upon it. Which Sussex resort did he create?

2. St Thomas's Day (December 21st) was traditionally a day for dispensing charity. What was the day's other name?

3. The font at North Mundham church is one of the largest in Sussex, and it's made of Sussex marble. What *is* Sussex marble?

4. What was the original function of the building which is now Brighton General Hospital?

5. If Sussex folk said they'd seen 'the pharisees', what were they referring to?

6. The county was once referred to as 'Silly Sussex'. What did this mean?

7. Where was the Roman army based in Sussex after the conquest of AD 43?

8. This is the only port between Dover and Portsmouth accessible at all states of the tide for vessels of up to four metres draft.

9. The Normans divided Sussex into six administrative areas running from east to west. They weren't counties or parishes: what *were* they called?

10. Name the only open prison in Sussex.

9. INDUSTRY

Nearly sixty years work in the jolly old forge,
Sometimes pleasant, sometimes rough,
Trying to please horses and horsemen,
It's made me jolly well tough.

(From 'The Song of the Blacksmith' by
Gaius Carley of Adversane)

1. Our neolithic forebears worked mines at Cissbury and at other sites along the Downs. What were they digging for?

2. Complete the rhyme:

   Master Huggett and his man John
   They did cast the first _____

3. Several ponds not far from Battle Abbey provided the power supply for an industry which thrived in the area from 1676 until 1874. What was produced there?

4. What did Thomas Brassey construct across five continents?

5. Which Lewes business celebrated its bicentenary in 1990?

6. It was completed in 1841, has 37 arches and is 1,475 ft long. What is it?

7. Which town's brickyards supplied 14,400 bricks and two thousand tiles for the building of Stanmer house in the early eighteenth century?

8. What was William Catt's area of expertise?

9. Which industry provided Hailsham's nineteenth century prosperity?

10. What was discovered at Heathfield in 1895 while engineers were looking for water?

10. A QUESTION OF SPORT

'Me bowling, Pilch batting and Box keeping wicket.'

(Most cricket lovers have their ideal teams, and these were the chief ingredients for the great Fred Lillywhite, who was born at Westhampnett and is buried there)

1. What was traditionally played in Sussex on Good Friday?

2. Which town was the first in England to organise motor racing trials?

3. A greyhound trained at Albourne achieved a world record on December 9th, 1986, by completing his 32nd straight win. What was his name?

4. Another famous runner, born October 9th 1955, in Brighton.

5. He was probably the greatest-ever all-rounder, playing football and cricket for England and holding the world long-jump record for 21 years. In 1901 he made six consecutive centuries.

6. Where was the first-ever test match played between England and Australia?

7. The poet John Keats came to a sporting event in Sussex in 1828 to take his mind off the death of his brother. What was the sport?

8. What happened as a consequence of the 36-round bout at Wadhurst in 1863 between Tom King and the American John Heenan?

9. Major W.W. Grantham was responsible for the revival this century of a sport now played only in Sussex and neighbouring counties.

10. Where the Royals come to play in Sussex.

11. INVENTORS

*A celebration of 'ingenurious'
men - as Sussex dialect speakers
might have described them.*

1. His inventions included a 'parlour telegraph' for domestic communications and remote detonators for under-water mines, but he's best known for building the first electric railway in Britain.

2. John Pell, born in Southwick in 1611, was a mathematical prodigy who's credited with inventing a sign which is still in use today. Which one?

3. A plaque in Middle street, Brighton, records that William Friese-Greene carried out his early experiments here. In what field?

4. Frederick Stanley Mockford, the air radio pioneer, is buried in Selmeston churchyard. Which call did he originate?

5. In which Sussex town did John Logie Baird transmit the first television pictures?

6. There's a memorial to Edmund Cartwright in Battle church. What did he invent?

7. James Starley was brought up at Albourne but later moved to Coventry. What kind of machines did he invent?

8. Robert Whitehead (1813-1905) is buried in the tranquil churchyard at Worth. His invention was rather less peaceful. What was it?

9. Joseph Aloysius Hansom patented the famous cab beloved of Sherlock Holmes. Which Sussex landmark did he design?

10. This famous twentieth century engineer lived at West Wittering. His name is best known hyphenated with another which begins with the same letter.

12. TOWNS

'Dear little Bognor!'
— Princess Victoria, who stayed in the town
before her accession

'Bugger Bognor!'
— last words attributed to George V. who
nevertheless gave the town its Regis suffix

1. Which resort town became, in 1901, the first in England to sanction mixed bathing?

2. Which town has two cliff lifts?

3. Which town boasts the motto *Progress?*

4. The river Wellsbourne runs through here.

5. There's a bandstand in the shopping precinct.

6. St John's Common lay at the heart of the present-day town.

7. Elementary, my dear Watson!

8. Where 'the guinea pigs' were treated during the second world war.

9. Hanging fairs were once common here.

10. In which town did Oscar Wilde write *The Importance of Being Earnest?*

13. VILLAGES

*Away to Sweet Felpham, for Heaven is
    there;
The Ladder of Angels descends thro'
    the air;
On the Turret its spiral does softly
    descend,
Thro' the village then winds, at My Cot
    it does end.*

(Lines written by William Blake, who lived at
    Felpham for three years from 1800)

1. In which West Sussex village is there
   a thatched well?

2. *'Who carried Christ speed thee today
   And lift thy heart up all the way'*

   Where will you find a roadside St Christopher with this inscription?

3. Which village church has a Saxon sundial inscribed with the name
   EADRIC?

4. Ticehurst lies close to the largest expanse of inland water in south-
   east England. What is it?

5. It has a Palladian church built by a Bishop of Durham.

6. What will you see next to the Shepherd and Dog pub in Fulking?

7. Sir Edward Dalyngrigge built the castle here in 1386.

8. Where a house sits over the entrance to a railway tunnel.

9. Which famous historian is buried at Fletching?

10. Cornelis Roetmans, who is buried at Playden, was Flemish. What
    was his trade?

14. FOLKLORE

'Here's to thee, old apple tree,
May'st thou bud, may'st thou blow,
May'st thou bear apples enow!'

(the toast drunk on Apple Howling Day, when boys
joined hands round the apple trees to encourage a good
crop the following year)

1. Who was sawn in half on Groaning Bridge?

2. A monster lived in a pond at Lyminster. What was it called?

3. St Wilfrid brought Christianity to Sussex. What is he supposed to have taught the natives to do?

4. If you offended the community in days gone by, you were likely to have a procession of villagers outside your house, making a commotion with improvised percussion instruments. This was sometimes known as 'skimmington' - but what was its more common Sussex name?

5. On March 1st the people of Arundel used to go to the bridge and shake themselves. Why?

6. May 29th was Oak Apple Day, but it had a more colourful name reflecting the punishment meted out to people who failed to 'sport their oak'. What was it?

7. Which craftsmen had their feast on St Crispin's Day?

8. And who celebrated on Old Clem Night?

9. Where did an old lady trick the Devil into fleeing?

10. And which saint took the Devil by the nose?

15. DES RES: A TOUR OF THE COUNTY'S GRANDER PROPERTIES

If I ever become a rich man,
Or if ever I grow to be old,
I will build a house with deep thatch
To shelter me from the cold,
And there shall the Sussex songs
be sung
And the story of Sussex told.

(Hilaire Belloc, The South Country)

1. The Duke of Wellington rejected the offer of this house because the hill was too steep.

2. A curse is said to have been responsible for its destruction.

3. The mosaics here include Venus & the Gladiators and Ganymede & the Eagle.

4. Its deer park stretches over 700 acres.

5. Which architect transformed the Royal Pavilion at Brighton into the oriental extravaganza we know today?

6. Which house was designed by Philip Webb, a friend of William Morris, several of whose wallpaper designs can be seen there?

7. The home of the Gage family since the fifteenth century.

8. The home of the Earls of Bessborough.

9. It's really two houses in one, because a medieval hall house from Kent was attached to the original property in 1910.

10. The long gallery here is so extensive that the yeomanry used it for drill practice in Napoleonic times.

16. PUBS

*Good ale, thou art my darling,
Thou art my joy both night and
morning!*

(traditional song)

1. Which public house is named after a disaster on Christmas Eve 1836?

2. Complete the strange name of the Yapton pub: *The Shoulder of Mutton and* . . . .

3. Firle once had four pubs: the Polecat, the Ram, the Woolpack and the Beanstalk. Only one survives. Which is it?

4. In which pub is there a pair of mummified cats on display?

5. The Anchor at Hartfield was originally built for another purpose. What was it?

6. Which famous political writer polished his debating skills at the White Hart, Lewes?

7. 'The first railway in the south of England' was built at Offham. What's the name of the pub in whose garden the railway tunnel can still be seen?

8. A pub sign at Westergate shows a white woman bathing a black baby. What's the name of the pub?

9. From which East Sussex inn did Hilaire Belloc set out on his walk across Sussex, celebrated in his book *The Four Men?*

10. It was the headquarters of the brutal Hawkhurst Gang.

17. MISCELLANEOUS

A round dedicated to Samuel Jeake, who lived at Rye in the seventeenth century. His learning embraced astrology, rhetoric, logic, poetry, natural philosophy, arithmetic, geography, geology, theology, drawing, heraldry, history, Latin, Greek and Hebrew.

1. Where will you find village stocks made of iron?

2. The house for the village pump at Willingdon has a distinctive form of decoration. What's been set among the flints on either side of the entrance?

3. What did Thomas Tipper brew at Newhaven?

4. What did John Tapsell design?

5. 'The exceeding beauty of the earth, in her splendour of life, yields a new thought with every petal' - so wrote a Victorian nature writer who's buried in Broadwater Cemetery. Who was he?

6. Coleman's Hatch, Plaw Hatch, Chuck Hatch... Why all the hatches on the edge of Ashdown Forest?

7. What's a Sussex twitten?

8. There are four villages called Marden in West Sussex. North, East and West are three of them. What's the fourth?

9. What's unusual about Walter Budd's tombstone at Dragon's Green?

10. There are two market crosses in Sussex, the most impressive being at Chichester. Where's the other?

18. ROYALTY

'The people are very indiscreet and troublesome here really, which makes this place quite a prison.'

(Queen Victoria on Brighton and the Royal Pavilion: she abandoned it for Osborne on the Isle of Wight)

1. Which steep street is the Prince Regent said to have driven down in a coach-and-four for a wager?

2. A statue which once stood outside St Paul's Cathedral was brought to Baldslow, near Hastings, by the writer Augustus Hare. Which monarch does it represent?

3. What did Elizabeth I leave under an oak tree at Northiam?

4. On the Downs between Plumpton and Westmeston is an unusual celebration of Queen Victoria's diamond jubilee. What is it?

5. Which king came ashore in a storm at Rye and stood godfather to the mayor's son?

6. King John came ashore on March 25, 1199, to claim the throne. Where did he land?

7. What have the following in common: William Cawley, John Downes, William Goffe, Gregory Norton, Peregrine Pelham, Anthony Stapley and James Temple?

8. Which Romano British king lived at Fishbourne?

9. This hotel is named after a monarch who stayed at the new resort before ascending the throne.

10. George IV married her - and then disowned her.

19. WRITERS

You came, and looked, and loved
  the view
Long known and loved by me,
Green Sussex fading into blue
With one grey glimpse of sea.

  Alfred Lord Tennyson, who lived
  at Black Down

1. Whose creations played on Ashdown Forest?

2. She lived at Rodmell and drowned in the Ouse.

3. Complete this couplet by Hilaire Belloc, who lived at Shipley -

   When I am dead, I hope it may be said:
   His sins were scarlet, but . . . .

4. Lamb House, Rye, was the home of the American-born novelist Henry James and, after his death in 1916, of another writer who used the town as the setting for a number of light novels. Who was he?

5. Which famous writer lived in a former Sussex iron master's house?

6. Tennyson spent his last years at Black Down, but he had lived in Sussex before, just after his marriage. In which West Sussex village?

7. George Moore's best known novel, *Esther Waters,* is set in a West Sussex village not far from Shoreham. Which one?

8. Which famous seventeenth century diarist laid one of the foundation stones of South Malling church?

9. *'Oh! a melancholy thing it is to deprive oneself of reason, and even to render ourselves beasts!'*

   Which Sussex diarist had trouble controlling his drinking habit?

10. Mark Lemon, who lived at Crawley, was the first editor of a famous magazine. Which one?

20. UNNATURAL DEATHS

Buryed Thomas Baker of West Dean who was found dead and frozen stiff in ye snow sitting withinside of ye Haven wall leading from Pevensea.

(*Pevensey parish register, January 31st, 1708*)

1. Who was on the throne when the Lewes martyrs were burned at the stake?

2. *Harold Rex interfectus est.* What do these Latin words mean?

3. In 1742 a Rye butcher named Breeds attempted to kill the mayor, Thomas Lamb, but murdered someone else by mistake. Breeds was arrested after going round the town shouting a self-incriminating slogan. What was it?

4. John George Haigh committed a series of gruesome murders at Crawley in the late 1940s. What did they become known as?

5. What was the name of the lifeboat which foundered off Rye Harbour in November 1928 with the loss of all 17 men aboard?

6. John Boots was killed at Newick in May 1737 in unusual circumstances. What was he doing?

7. 'Mrs Shepherd, Mistress of the Red Lion public house at Crowborough', was killed by something thrown in her pub on June 26th, 1796. What hit her?

8. Daniel Skayles, his tombstone at Patcham records, was 'unfortunately shot' on the evening of November 7th, 1796. What was he doing at the time?

9. Sarah Ann French of Chiddingly poisoned her husband in 1852 because of her love for another man. What did she cook him?

10. Nine-year-old John Archdeacon's gravestone outside All Saints Church, Hastings, relates that he died after being beaten by an angry man. What had he done to infuriate him?

21. ROGUES & ECCENTRICS

*'Wunt be druv,' is the obstinate Sussex
motto. Here are some characters
who took individuality to colourful or
illegal extremes...*

1. He was a patron of surrealist artists, a designer of weird buildings in the Mexican jungle and the founder of an arts college in West Sussex.

2. A rebel who was killed by Alexander Iden.

3. Dr Richard Russell was the man whose seawater cure did much to encourage visitors to Brighton in the eighteenth century, but another Richard Russell was sent to gaol in 1796 at the tender age of 13. What had he done?

4. 'Mad Jack' Fuller MP, famous for his folly building, was massively built and weighed 20 stone. What, therefore, did his enemies call him?

5. John Olliver's tomb can be seen on the downs west of Worthing. What was his business?

6. Who disappeared without trace on November 7th, 1974, having last been seen at Uckfield?

7. He was called 'the wickedest man in the world' and preached the gospel of 'do what thou wilt'. He died in Hastings on December 5th, 1947. Who was he?

8. George Bristow was the man at the centre of the Hastings Rarities scandal. What did he do for a living?

9. Charles Dawson, a solicitor and clerk to the Uckfield magistrates, was involved in another Sussex-based scandal. Which one?

10. This MP was a noted orator, a Sussex squire and the owner of the magazine John Bull. He was sentenced to seven years' penal servitude for his Victory Bonds fraud after the first world war.

22. GOD'S CREATURES

'One-erum, two-erum, cock-erum, shu-erum,
sith-erum, sath-erum, wineberry, wagtail,
tarry-diddle, den.'

(the Sussex shepherds' way of counting sheep)

1. John Ellman, who lived at Glynde, developed a notable Sussex breed. What was it?

2. What did the old lady let out of her bag every April 14th at Heathfield?

3. The naturalist Gilbert White got to know Timothy when he visited his aunt in Ringmer. What *was* Timothy?

4. The geologist Gideon Mantell discovered the fossil bones of a then unknown prehistoric beast near Balcombe. Which one?

5. Downland shepherds used to earn good money from trapping these birds, which were regarded as a culinary delicacy.

6. Which animal was hunted every November 30th when the people went 'Andring'?

7. It was a Sussex custom to share news of births, deaths and marriages with these useful creatures.

8. Rosslyn Bruce, the eccentric rector of Herstmonceux from 1923-1956, was an animal fanatic who, among other things, bred a strange mouse. What was odd about it?

9. A brass plate in the square at Battle marks the spot where animals were tethered. Which animals, and why?

10. Lady Monckton, who lived at Folkington, introduced a bill in Parliament to protect this animal.

23. CHURCHES

If every year for seven years
A hundred thousand men
Gave sixty pence and sixty prayers,
From weald and down and den,
All dwellers in our Sussex towns
Would have their churches then!

(Bishop George Bell -
Song of the Sussex Church Builders)

1. The Teise stream runs alongside the most impressive monastic remains in Sussex. Which?

2. Where will you find a church permanently divided in two, with Anglican worship on one side and Roman Catholic on the other?

3. Which church has a pulpit shaped like a Galilean ship's prow?

4. Egdean, Twineham, East Guldeford: what do these three churches have in common?

5. Which Sussex church stands highest above sea level?

6. Which East Sussex church has more than thirty cast iron grave slabs set into its floor?

7. Which West Sussex church displays a rare example of a vamping horn?

8. What happened in Chichester on February 21st, 1861?

9. What's the distinctive feature of St Michael's, Lewes, and the nearby churches at Southease and Piddinghoe?

10. Only one church in Britain has an original Saxon rhenish helm. Where is it?

24. BATTLES

For the Sussex stock is staunch,
And the Sussex blood is true,
And the Sussex lads are keen
When there's soldiers' work to do.
Hear us tramp, tramp, tramp
Till the country is a camp,
And we start the little business
We have sworn to carry through.

(Marching song written by A.W. Busbridge for 'Lowther's Lambs' - the Southdown Battalions of the Royal Sussex Regiment raised by Lt Col Claude Lowther of Herstmonceux Castle during the first world war)

1. Thomas Lord Camoys, whose retinue was made up entirely of Sussex men, was made a Knight of the Garter after a famous battle on October 25th, 1415. Which one?

2. What happened at Senlac?

3. Who defeated Henry III at the Battle of Lewes in 1264?

4. The so-called 'Battle of Lewes Road' was fought in Brighton during the 1920s. It was part of a wider conflict. Which one?

5. How many ships were the citizens of Rye required to provide for the defence of England against the Spanish Armada in 1588?

6. The 70-gun *Anne* was one of eight ships lost by the English in a joint Anglo-Dutch battle with the French in June, 1690. What name is given to that battle?

7. A folly was raised at Heathfield in memory of the exploits of General George Elliott. What did he do?

8. Lieutenant-General Thomas Gage of Firle was recalled in disgrace after a bloody battle during the American War of Independence. Which one?

9. Legend says that, after the Battle of Poitiers in 1356, the young Sir John Pelham was given a token reward which later became the family's armorial emblem. What was it?

10. The 35th Regiment of Foot, later to become the Royal Sussex Regiment, discharged 'the most perfect volley ever fired on the battlefield' on September 13th, 1759 - and in so doing ensured that Britain, rather than the French, should possess a large piece of territory in the Americas. What was the battle?

25. MISCELLANEOUS

*Another 'soss-about' round, as a
dialect speaker might have it: 'to mix
different things together'. But beware -
the stupe may be middling vlothered!*

1. At one time there were three piers to be seen along Brighton seafront. The oldest of them was destroyed in a storm in December, 1896. What was it called?

2. The Sussex County Lunatic Asylum was opened in 1859. Where?

3. Haven Brow, Short Brow, Rough Brow, Brass Point, Flagstaff Point, Bailey's Brow, Went Hill Brow. How are they known collectively?

4. Which West Sussex village was renowned for its sheep fair?

5. Which East Sussex village was the centre of the trug-making industry?

6. The nature reserve at Kingley Vale, near Chichester, is famous for its forest of *taxus baccata*. Which tree is this?

7. Jack and Jill went *up* the hill to fetch their pail of water. If they lived under the Downs, what was their probable source of supply?

8. Born in Heyshott, he was a fierce campaigner against the Corn Laws. Who was he?

9. Who built Peacehaven?

10. The Bayeux Tapestry shows an ominous star passing over Sussex before the Battle of Hastings. What do we call it today?

26. COATS OF ARMS

Quarterly, 1st, Gules, a bend argent and on the bend an escutcheon Or, charged with a demi-lion rampant pierced through the mouth by an arrow within a double tressure flory counterflory gules; 2nd. Gules, three lions passant guardant in pale Or, in chief a label of three points argent; 3rd, Chequy Or and azure; 4th, Gules, a lion rampant Or.

(Arms of the Duke of Norfolk)

1. Martlets appear on both the East and West Sussex coats of arms. What's distinctive about these heraldic birds?

2. In 1992 a Sussex village became the first in England to be granted its own coat of arms. Which village was it?

3. The arms of the Duke of Richmond and Gordon show his descent from royalty. Which king fathered the illegitimate son who became the first Duke?

4. The crest of the Abergavenny family can be seen on buildings in the Eridge area. The device is an animal with a Tudor rose, a portcullis and a large 'A' tied with tassles. What's the animal?

5. Sir Henry Guldeford fought for King Ferdinand of Spain against the Moors and was knighted at Burgos. The Guldeford coat of arms, previously 'a saltire between four martlets', reflects this proud achievement. What was added to the shield?

Punning, or canting, is common on coats of arms:

6. What device appears on the arms of the Goring family?

7. The Earl of Chichester, descended from the Pelhams, has some large birds on his shield. What are they?

8. Which Sussex family has three whelk shells on its coat of arms?

9. Which animal's head appears on the arms of Viscount Hailsham?

10. Feathers adorn the arms of the family which lived at Uppark from 1747. What was their surname?

27. RAILWAYS

Swift as an arrow o'er the burning rail,
With mightiest movement motionless
we dart;
When sudden leaps aloft the screaming
wail,
As if a tortured giant burst his heart.

(Rev. C.A. Kennaway - The Tunnel at
Clayton, 1851)

What were the names of the lines which ran:

1. from Polegate to Eridge?

2. from Lewes to East Grinstead?

3. from Brighton to the Downs?

4. In which year was the London to Brighton railway line opened?

5. Twenty-three people were killed and nearly two hundred injured in a crash involving three trains in August 1861. Where?

6. A new rail service began on May 14th, 1984. What was it?

7. What fitting name was given to the new road built on the site of Henfield station after the line closed in 1966?

8. What type of business now operates at the old Singleton railway station?

9. Where in Sussex is the terminal station of the reconstructed Kent and East Sussex Railway?

10. In June 1881 Arthur Lefroy killed stockbroker Frederick Gold for his money in the carriage of a London-to-Brighton train. Where did the attack take place?

28. WINDMILLS

See you our little mill that clacks,
So busy by the brook?
She has ground her corn and paid her tax
Ever since Domesday Book

(Rudyard Kipling - Puck's Song)

1. There are three principal types of windmill, two of them being the post mill and the tower mill. What's the third?

2. Which writer owned Shipley mill?

3. Jack and Jill are a handsome pair side by side above Clayton. Which is black and which is white?

4. John Constable painted a distinctive East Sussex windmill that has barns built around it. Where is it?

5. Windmills were always moving and/or having their names changed. What did Rudyard Kipling call the one at Punnett's Town?

6. What are windmill sails called in Sussex?

7. Millers devised a language of sails so that customers a long way off would know whether, for instance, they had finished work for the day. Those at Polegate were placed in the St George Cross position in 1973. What did this signify?

8. What's believed to be the county's oldest post mill can be seen on Ashdown Forest. What's its name?

9. Where will you find a mill with windows shaped like wheels?

10. Which windmill is said to sit at the very centre of Sussex?

EAST SUSSEX PICTURE QUIZ

1. This is thought to be a crusader's tombstone. In which church will you find it?

2. A famous landmark. Where is it?

3. An ancient fortification. What's its name?

4. A working watermill. Where?

5. This ruined medieval dovecot adjoins a large barn. In which village?

6. An unusual village church. Where?

7. Who painted the pulpit?

8. This stone marks the visit of Elizabeth I to a well. In which town?

9. A church by a pond. Where?

10. The sheep give a clue to the whereabouts of this remote church. Which is it?

WEST SUSSEX PICTURE QUIZ

1. *'Be true and just in all your dealings'* reads the inscription on this stone. Where is it?

2. The yellow lines alongside this road disappear into the rising tide. Where are we?

3. The wording on this stone declares that the tenants of the manor have the right to draw water from the spring. In which village?

4. Which church is this?

5. This fine old building is a place of worship. What's its name?

•I•PRAY•GOD•BLES•MY•LORD•OF
•DORSET•AND•MY•LADIE•AND•AL
•THEIR•POSTERITIE•AND•DO•1619•

6. *'I pray God bles my Lord of Dorset and my ladie and al their posteritie.'* In which building will you find this inscription?

7. The inside of this church is photographed more often than the outside. Why?

8. Ruins by a river. Where?

9. An ancient door. In which church?

10. A distinctive shape. Where's this church?

ANSWERS

1. SUSSEX BOOK OF RECORDS

1. The Long Man of Wilmington. He's 230 ft tall.
2. Five ounces. It was the size of a tennis ball.
3. The mouse-eared bat. It was Britain's largest species, with a wing span of 18 inches.
4. St Bartholomew's in Brighton. It was built to the supposed dimensions of Noah's Ark and measures 140 ft to the top of the cross.
5. William Huskisson. The MP for Chichester was killed by Stephenson's Rocket on September 15th, 1830.
6. Black Down. It's 919 ft above sea level.
7. At Alciston. It's 170 ft long.
8. In Northiam. The house called Smugglers has one room upstairs and one down - but a family of five once lived there.
9. At Dell Quay, near Chichester. It was once reckoned to be the ninth busiest port on the country.
10. At Lullington. It's about 16 ft square and is the remnant of the chancel of a medieval church.

2. FAMOUS MEN

1. The Man Who Broke the Bank at Monte Carlo.
2. Grey Owl. He lived as a Red Indian in Canada and wrote several books about wildlife and conservation.
3. Pestalozzi, the Swiss educational theorist. The Pestalozzi Village is at Sedlescombe, near Battle.
4. Bognor Regis. Sir Richard, who died in 1799, spent a fortune in an attempt to create a fashionable watering-place there.
5. Gardening. He was known as 'The father of the English garden'.
6. Lancing, Ardingly and Hurstpierpoint colleges.
7. Massage. He was a 'shampooist', or hot baths proprietor, and personal masseur to the King.
8. Off Beachy Head. Engels often spent his holidays in Eastbourne.
9. Charles II. Captain Tettersell took the fugitive monarch to France on his coal brig, the *Surprise*.
10. Chanctonbury Ring.

3. THE ARTS

(The quotation by Angelica Garnett is taken from Deceived with Kindness: a Bloomsbury Childhood, *published by Oxford Paperbacks)*

1. Glyndebourne Opera House. His wife was the soprano Audrey Mildmay.
2. Sir Edward Burne-Jones. He lived in North End House.
3. Ralph Vaughan Williams. He compiled *The English Hymnal,* which contains tunes named after Sussex places, among them Rodmell, Horsham and Monk's Gate.
4. Pianos and other keyboard instruments.
5. Vaslav Nijinsky. He died here in 1950.
6. Sir Hubert Parry.
7. Vanessa Bell. With Duncan Grant and her son Quentin she painted the murals in Berwick church.
8. The Dodo House. The sculptor had never seen an ostrich!
9. On board the Titanic. A plaque near Eastbourne's bandstand records that her perished 'with others of the hero-musicians' on April 15th, 1912.
10. J.W.M. Turner.

4. CASTLES & OTHER DEFENCES

1. Lewes. But it's not known whether a keep was ever built on Brack Mount, north-east of the existing castle.
2. Martello towers. They were built along the coast of Kent and Sussex as a defence against Napoleonic invasion.
3. Arundel. The castle wasn't fully restored until 1800.
4. Bramber Castle, now a ruin.
5. Camber.
6. Hastings.
7. The Royal Military Canal. This moat, less than thirty feet wide, was designed to keep Napoleon's navy at bay.
8. They all have the ramparts of Iron Age hillforts on top of them.
9. Pevensey. The Roman walls still stand.
10. The A24, north of Dial Post.

5. FAMOUS WOMEN

(The epitaph to Elizabeth Blackwell is on the wall of her house in Exmouth Place, below Hastings Castle)

1. Kitty O'Shea. She and Charles Stewart Parnell were married in Steyning in 1891, but he died a few months later.
2. A dipper, or bathing-woman.
3. Roedean School. The sisters at first used houses in the town, the present building opening in 1899.
4. She dressed as a man in order to follow her lover to the wars.
5. In the absence of her husband, the constable, she successfully defended Pevensey Castle against a siege by Richard II.
6. Medicine. Elizabeth Blackwell, who overcame great prejudice, was the first woman to be placed on the British Medical Register. Sophia Jex Blake, one of her first students, was a pioneer in women's education.
7. Margaret Thatcher. Five people were killed when an IRA time-bomb exploded at the Grand Hotel, Brighton, on October 12th, 1984, during the week of the Conservative Party conference.
8. The Women's Institute.
9. Lady Hamilton, later Nelson's mistress. She was then Emma Hart, fifteen years old and the mistress of Sir Harry Fetherstonhaugh.
10. Dame Vera Lynn. 'The sweetheart of the forces', as she was known during the second world war, has lived in the village for many years.

6. SUSSEX DIALECT

(The Rev. Parish's dictionary was re-published by Gardner's of Bexhill in 1957, with additional entries by Helena Hall)

1. A decayed tooth. Toothache.
2. Completely tired out.
3. Be off with you!
4. Beer and gin.
5. The pansy.
6. That you're feeling idle. ('A mysterious individual,' wrote Parish, 'whose influence is supposed to produce indolence.')
7. A scarecrow.
8. Sulky.
9. Satiated. Glutted.
10. In a rage.

7. RELIGIOUS TYPES

(The lines by Minnie Louise Haskins are inscribed at the foot of the King's memorial window in the Royal Mausoleum at Windsor)

1. His left thumb. It was blown off when, as a nine-year-old, he tried to destroy a wasps' nest with a home-made bomb. He was known in Africa as 'One thumb white boss'.
2. *Good King Wenceslas.*
3. At Winchelsea. There's a plaque at the spot, by the churchyard wall.
4. In a cart. Legend says it broke down at Steyning, which is why he settled here. Christopher Fry based his play *The Boy with the Cart* on the story.
5. In Chichester Cathedral.
6. He was a Quaker.
7. Sinner Saved.
8. As a shoemaker. He came to Sussex from London in 1850.
9. The tuning of church bells.
10. Wagner (H.M. and A.D.)

8. MISCELLANEOUS

1. St Leonards.
2. Gooding Day.
3. A stone made of millions of compacted fossil snails.
4. It was the workhouse.
5. The fairies.
6. Happy, or blessed. From the Old English, *saelig.*
7. In Chichester.
8. Newhaven.
9. Rapes. There were five to begin with, but the westernmost was later split in two.
10. Ford.

9. INDUSTRY

(Gaius Carley also wrote his memoirs, published in 1963)

1. Flint. For tools and weapons.
2. Cannon. Ralph Hogge lived at Hogge House, Buxted, and his cannon were reputedly used against the Armada in 1588. The iron industry flourished in Sussex during the sixteenth and seventeenth centuries.
3. Gunpowder. There were some notable accidents: Sedlescombe powdermills blew up in December 1764, killing four men, and Battle Powderworks was destroyed in March, 1801.
4. Railways. He was partner of George Stephenson. He's buried at Catsfield.
5. Harvey's Brewery.
6. The Ouse Valley railway viaduct at Balcombe.
7. Burgess Hill, where brickmaking continues to this day.
8. Tide mills. He ran the Tide Mills operation, near Bishopstone, in the mid-nineteenth century.
9. Rope-making. At one time there were eight ropewalks in the town.
10. Natural gas. It was used to light the railway station until the 1930s.

10. A QUESTION OF SPORT

1. Marbles.
2. Bexhill, in 1902.
3. Ballyregan Bob. The race was at Hove stadium.
4. Steve Ovett, the Olympic gold medallist.
5. C.B. Fry. The great Sussex batsman scored 3,147 runs in 1901. Apart from his sporting prowess, he was a schoolmaster, journalist, broadcaster and novelist - and he declined the throne of Albania!
6. At Sheffield Park. The first Earl of Sheffield was a passionate cricket supporter, and the visiting Australians always used to begin their tour of England by playing Lord Sheffield's XI.
7. Prize-fighting. He watched a bout between Jack Randall, 'the Nonpareil' and Ned Turner, 'the Out-and-Outer', at Crawley Down. Randall won by a knock-out.
8. Prize-fighting was made illegal. King won after 36 rounds, and the brutality of the affair outraged the general public.
9. Stoolball.
10. Cowdray. For polo in the park.

11. INVENTORS

1. Magnus Volk. He's buried at Ovingdean.
2. ÷
3. Cinematography.
4. Mayday.
5. Hastings. There's a plaque in Queen's Arcade, near the town hall.
6. The power loom.
7. Bicycles. One of his inventions was the Social Trycycle which inspired the music hall song: *You'll look sweet Upon the seat Of a bicycle made for two.*
8. The first successful torpedo.
9. Arundel Cathedral.
10. Sir Henry Royce of Rolls-Royce fame.

12. TOWNS

1. Bexhill on Sea
2. Hastings.
3. Littlehampton.
4. Brighton. It rises at Patcham and used to run, in winter, along Marlborough Place to Pool Valley. It was piped into a wooden sewer in 1796.
5. Crawley. The bandstand came from the former racecourse at Gatwick.
6. Burgess Hill.
7. Crowborough. Sir Arthur Conan Doyle, Sherlock Holmes' creator, spent the last 23 years of his life at Windlesham Manor.
8. East Grinstead. The 'guinea pigs' were injured servicemen who underwent plastic surgery at the Queen Victoria Hospital during the second world war.
9. Horsham. The fairs coincided with public hangings at the county gaol, the last of them on April 6th, 1844.
10. Worthing. The play's chief character is named after the town.

13. VILLAGES

1. East Marden.
2. At Treyford.
3. Bishopstone.
4. Bewl Water. The reservoir was completed in 1975 and holds 6,900 million gallons of water.
5. Glynde. The bishop was a member of the Trevor family who lived at Glynde Place.
6. A natural spring.
7. Bodiam. The castle was begun in 1385 as a protection against French raiders.
8. Clayton.
9. Edward Gibbon, who wrote *The Decline and Fall of the Roman Empire.*
10. A brewer. His grave slab is inscribed with two casks and a crossed mashstick and fork.

14. FOLKLORE

1. The Brede Giant, Sir Goddard Oxenbridge. There was a *real* Sir Goddard, but the legendary one was a cannibal. The children of Sussex got him drunk and sawed him in half.
2. The Knucker. A deep pond near the church is called the Knucker Hole.
3. To fish.
4. Rough music.
5. It rid them of fleas for the rest of the year.
6. Pinch Bum Day.
7. Cobblers.
8. Blacksmiths.
9. At Devil's Dyke. He mistook her candle for the rising sun, and fled.
10. St Dunstan, a blacksmith by trade. The Devil suffered so badly at his hands that he vowed never to enter a house with a horseshoe over its door.

15. DES RES

1. Uppark. The nation had offered Wellington a country estate in gratitude for the victory of Waterloo. He declined Uppark, saying that he had crossed the Alps once and didn't intend repeating the experience for the rest of his life.
2. Cowdray. The family which owned it had been granted Battle Abbey at the Dissolution, and an angry monk is said to have foretold that the line would perish by fire and water. The house burned down in 1793, and the last Viscount Montague drowned a week later.
3. Bignor Roman Villa.
4. Petworth House.
5. John Nash.
6. Standen, near East Grinstead.
7. Firle Place.
8. Stansted Park, west of Chichester.
9. Great Dixter, Northiam.
10. Parham Park, near Storrington.

16. PUBS

1. The Snowdrop at Lewes. Eight people died in Britain's worst avalanche disaster.
2. Cucumbers.
3. The Ram.
4. The Stag Inn, All Saints Street, Hastings.
5. A workhouse for women.
6. Thomas Paine, author of *Rights of Man*. He influenced the makers of the American and French revolutions.
7. The Chalkpit. Carriages full of chalk from the pit descended the steep incline to be loaded into barges at a wharf alongside a cut from the River Ouse.
8. The Labour in Vain.
9. The George at Robertsbridge.
10. The Mermaid Inn at Rye.

17. MISCELLANEOUS

1. At Ninfield.
2. Cows' knuckle bones.
3. 'The best old stingo', according to his gravestone.
4. An unusual kind of gate which pivots on a central pillar. There are tapsell gates at Friston, East Dean and Jevington in East Sussex, and at Pyecombe and Coombes in West Sussex.
5. Richard Jefferies.
6. The word means 'gate', and these were entry points to the forest.
7. A narrow alley between walls or hedges.
8. Up.
9. It stands in a pub garden.
10. At Alfriston.

18. ROYALTY

1. Keere Street in Lewes.
2. Queen Anne. It stands in the garden of Hare's country mansion, Holmhurst, which is now a convent.
3. Her shoes of green damask silk.
4. A plantation of trees in a 'V' shape.
5. George I, on January 3rd, 1726. The boy was named George.
6. At Shoreham.
7. They were the Sussex men who signed Charles I's death warrant.
8. Cogidubnus.
9. The Royal Victoria Hotel at St Leonards.
10. Maria Fitzherbert. Mrs Fitzherbert, twice widowed and a Roman Catholic, was married to the Prince of Wales on December 15th, 1785. It was, however, an illegal ceremony because The Royal Marriages Act decreed that no descendant of George II could marry without the monarch's permission. The Church recognised the marriage, but George later married his cousin, Princess Caroline of Brunswick.

19. WRITERS

1. A.A. Milne's. He lived at Hartfield, and Pooh & Co played at 'an enchanted place' on the forest.
2. Virginia Woolf.
3. '. . . . his books were read.'
4. E.F. Benson, author of the Mapp & Lucia books.
5. Rudyard Kipling. At Bateman's, Burwash.
6. Warninglid. But he wasn't happy there: services were poor, a wall was blown down in a storm and he learned that a baby had been buried somewhere in the house.
7. Upper Beeding.
8. John Evelyn.
9. Thomas Turner. There's a plaque on his house at East Hoathly.
10. *Punch.* He lived at Vine Cottage from 1858 until his death in 1870, was a friend of Charles Dickens and was known as The Father of Crawley.

20. UNNATURAL DEATHS

1. Queen Mary.
2. King Harold was killed. The words appear on the Bayeux Tapestry.
3. 'Butchers should kill Lambs!'
4. The acid bath murders. Haigh ran a plastic finger nail factory in Leopold Road and immersed the bodies of his victims in concentrated sulphuric acid.
5. *The Mary Stanford.*
6. Playing cricket. The parish register recorded that he was killed 'by running against another man on crossing wicket'.
7. A skittles ball. *The Sussex Weekly Advertiser* reported that as she was 'crossing her ninepin alley, where some men were at play, she was unhappily struck by the bowl on the temple, which. . . fractured her skull in the most shocking manner'.
8. Smuggling. He was shot by a customs officer when his gang was caught red-handed.
9. An onion pie. She put arsenic in it and was hanged for murder.
10. He had teased the man's mule.

21. ROGUES & ECCENTRICS

1. Edward James, who died in 1984, had inherited 20 million dollars and the West Dean Estate.
2. Jack Cade. He led a rebellion in 1450, and his fate is recorded on a memorial at Cade Street, near Heathfield.
3. He was a highwayman. He robbed the Hurst Green Mail, but was given a sentence of only six months 'in consideration of his tender age'.
4. The Hippopotamus.
5. He was a miller.
6. Lord Lucan. He had killed his children's nanny, probably mistaking her for his estranged wife.
7. Aleister Crowley.
8. He was a taxidermist. The 'rarities' were birds supposedly found in Sussex, stuffed by Bristow, passed to the authorities and added to the official List of British Birds. Ornithologists later became suspicious, however, and several specimens were struck off the list.
9. The Piltdown Man hoax. Dawson broke news of the find to the Geological Society in 1912, and the skull was accepted as genuine until the early 1950s.
10. Horatio Bottomley. He built stables and a racecourse next to his house at Upper Dicker.

22. GOD'S CREATURES

1. The Southdown sheep.
2. A cuckoo. The Heffle (Heathfield) or Cuckoo Fair was held from 1315 until the second world war.
3. A tortoise. You can see him on the village sign at Ringmer. The British Museum has his shell.
4. The iguanodon.
5. Wheatears, also known as ortolans.
6. The squirrel.
7. Bees.
8. It was green!
9. Bulls, for baiting.
10. Badgers.

23. CHURCHES

(Bishop Bell, whose poem heads this round of questions, was Bishop of Chichester from 1929 to 1958. His memorial in Chichester Cathedral records that he was 'a true pastor, poet and patron of the arts, champion of the oppressed and tireless worker for Christian unity')

1. Bayham Abbey.
2. At Arundel. The former chancel of the parish church belongs to the (Roman Catholic) Duke of Norfolk and can be entered only from the castle grounds.
3. St Leonard's parish church.
4. They were built of Tudor brick. Most of Egdean's original bricks disappeared during Victorian restoration work.
5. Fairlight. The village is nearly 600 ft above sea level.
6. Wadhurst. This was a centre of the iron industry.
7. Ashurst. It's a kind of musical instrument.
8. The cathedral spire collapsed.
9. They have round towers.
10. At Sompting.

24. BATTLES

1. Agincourt. Lord Camoys died in 1420 and is buried at Trotton.
2. It was the site of the Battle of Hastings.
3. Simon de Montfort.
4. The General Strike of 1926. When middle-class volunteers attempted to drive trams from the Lewes Road depot, strikers and their families resisted them. The strikers were then charged by mounted police, and twenty-two of them were later imprisoned for their part in what became a pitched battle.
5. One. She was hired from a Captain Russell, and put to sea on May 6th, 1588, with a complement of fifty men and five boys.
6. The Battle of Beachy Head.
7. He defended Gibraltar against the siege by France and Spain between 1779 and 1783. The Gibraltar Tower stands in Heathfield Park.
8. The Battle of Bunker Hill, June 17th, 1775. General Gage was commander-in-chief of the British forces, which took the hill but at a very high cost in deaths and injuries.
9. A buckle. It appears on many buildings and on the 'Bow Bells' milestones between Uckfield and Horsebridge on the A22.
10. The Battle of Quebec. General James Wolfe was mortally wounded in the British assault on the Heights of Abraham which decided the fate of Canada.

25. MISCELLANEOUS

1. The Chain Pier.
2. At Haywards Heath. It later became St Francis Hospital.
3. As the Seven Sisters, the towering cliffs between Cuckmere Haven and Birling Gap.
4. Findon.
5. Herstmonceux.
6. The yew.
7. A dew pond.
8. Richard Cobden, leader of the Anti-Corn-Law League in the 1840s. The Corn Laws were repealed in 1846.
9. Charles Neville. He bought the land in 1914 and was also responsible for the early development of Telscombe Cliffs and Saltdean.
10. Halley's Comet.

26. COATS OF ARMS

1. They have no feet.
2. Henfield. The College of Arms granted the crest after researching the village's history. It was presented by the then Lord Lieutenant of Sussex, the Duke of Richmond and Gordon.
3. Charles II.
4. A bull.
5. A pomegranate.
6. A ring. Three of them, in fact.
7. Pelicans.
8. The Shelleys. The poet, Percy Bysshe Shelley, was a member of this family.
9. A hog. The last holder of the title was Quentin Hogg MP, who renounced it in 1963 in order to remain in the House of Commons: he had some hope of becoming leader of the Conservative Party. In 1970 he was created a life peer and took the title of Lord Hailsham of St Marylebone.
10. Fetherstonhaugh.

27. RAILWAYS

1. The Cuckoo Line.
2. The Bluebell Line.
3. The Devil's Dyke Railway.
4. In 1841.
5. In the Clayton Tunnel, on August 25th, 1861. Most of the dead were on a Sunday excursion train. As a result of the accident, the signalling system was thoroughly overhauled.
6. The Gatwick Express, between Gatwick Airport and Victoria.
7. Beechings. The line was a victim of the nationwide cuts introduced by Lord Beeching. Similarly, there's a Beeching Way at East Grinstead.
8. A vineyard.
9. At Bodiam.
10. In the Balcombe Tunnel. Lefroy was hanged on November 29th, 1881.

28. WINDMILLS

1. The smock mill. The name comes from its resemblance to the former farm labourer's costume. It has a rigid, wooden body and a rotating cap.
2. Hilaire Belloc.
3. Jack is black.
4. At West Blatchington, Hove.
5. Cherry Black, though it's actually known as either Cherry Clack or Blackdown mill. It once stood among cherry orchards in Kent.
6. Sweeps.
7. It was the sign of mourning. Ephraim Ovenden was the last miller. By the time of his death, in 1973, he had sold the mill to Eastbourne and District Preservation Trust, which marked his passing in a fitting manner.
8. Nutley Mill. Its restoration won an Architectural Heritage Year award in 1975.
9. At Stone Cross, near Eastbourne.
10. Chailey smock mill, also known as the Heritage mill.

EAST SUSSEX PICTURE QUIZ

1. St Peter, Bexhill. It dates from the thirteenth century, and is mounted on the north wall of the tower.
2. Brighton. The clock tower at the junction of North Street, West Street and Queen's Road.
3. The Ypres Tower, at Rye. It was built in 1250 as a defence against French raiders.
4. At Michelham Priory, Upper Dicker.
5. Alciston.
6. Glynde.
7. Duncan Grant, to designs by his daughter, Angelica. It's in Berwick Church.
8. Rye. The well is in the garden of a private house in Deadmans Lane.
9. At Friston. The tapsell gate can be seen on the right.
10. East Guldeford, on Romney marsh.

WEST SUSSEX PICTURE QUIZ

1. On the bridge at Arundel. This was the heartfelt comment of the mayor, William Holmes, who felt let down by his colleagues over a scheme to widen the bridge in 1828.
2. At Bosham.
3. Albourne. The stone is set into the wall of Spring Cottage in Church Lane.
4. Climping. It has remarkable Norman carving around the doorway and the window above it.
5. The Blue Idol. It's a Quaker meeting house at Coneyhurst.
6. In Sackville College, East Grinstead.
7. Because of its renowned medieval wall paintings. This is Hardham church.
8. At Arundel. These are the remains of a medieval friary near the bridge.
9. Steyning.
10. At Warminghurst.

Front Cover: John 'Mad Jack' Fuller had the pyramid erected in Brightling churchyard as his mausoleum.

Back Cover: Arundel Castle, taken from the friary ruins *(see West Sussex picture quiz no. 8)*.